# The Essence of Winners
## A Roadmap to Arriving!

Herman Cajigas Jr. (HCJ)
Copyright © 2025 by Herman Cajigas Jr.
All rights reserved

Herman Cajigas Jr.
*The Essence of Winners*
A Roadmap to Arriving!
P.O. Box 940551
Miami. FL 33194

Or fax your request to (305) 220-2666 on official letterhead.
ISBN 979-8-218-55472-9 (Paperback)

Cover Design by Herman Cajigas Jr.
First Edition 1/12/2025
Printed in the USA

# *The Essence of Winners*

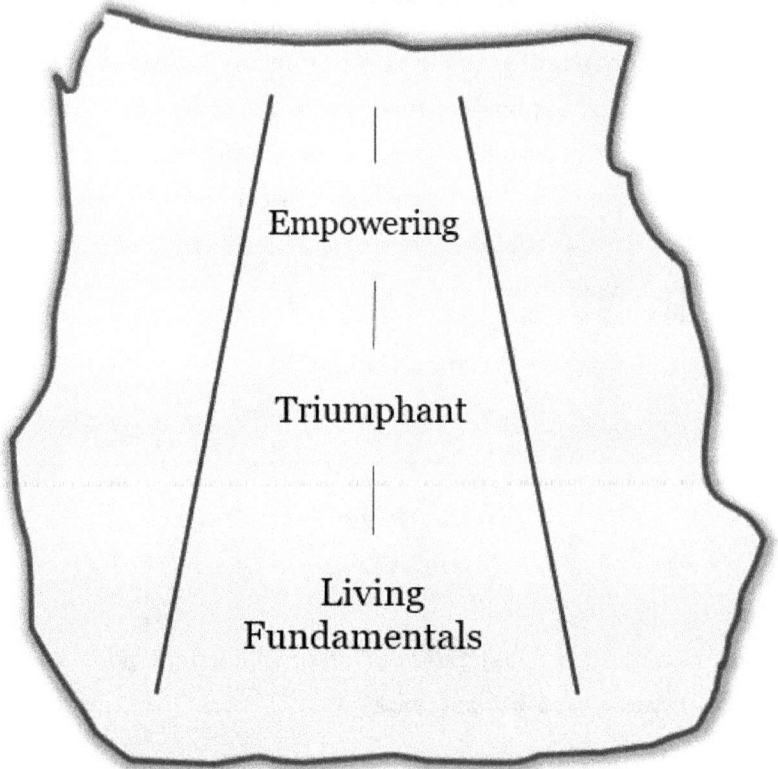

Empowering

Triumphant

Living
Fundamentals

## A Roadmap to Arriving!

Herman Cajigas Jr. (HCJ)

# Table of Content

# Acknowledgment

To all the people who have played a role in my life and made this book possible, thank you for your care, support, and encouragement.

# Dedication

This book is dedicated to my wife, parents, family, and friends whose examples of integrity, values, morals, and work ethic set the standard I strive to live for. May God bless their lives and souls.

# Introduction

Today, we are being assailed by political, social, and economic division, turmoil, and unrest that is tearing at the fabric and moral integrity of our individual lives, educational and legal institutions, government, and country.

This book shares a compilation of principles, concepts, quotes, and supporting stories that are the *"essence"* of living an empowered, successful life. It attempts to remind us of our esteemed past and, more importantly, our bright future if we stop the madness. Its title, "The Essence of Winners," refers to the characteristics, values (goals, ideals, opinions), and virtues (integral standards) shared by successful, thriving individuals and our path to future greatness.

The book not only expresses the author's point of view, but the author now wishes to give credit to all external contributing content denoted throughout the text, including other writers' quotes and stories, artificial intelligence, and internet-based definitions.

It is not rocket science. But for our present culture, the substance of the prose shared throughout these writings highlights the importance of ascribing or adhering to enriching foundational basics, loosely categorized throughout the book as *empowering, triumphant,* and *living fundamentals.*

For those who already excel in their lives, the work serves as a reminder of the convictions and building blocks that help one have a rewarding journey. And for all who struggle to make sense of their path in life, the collective worth of the ideas, lore, and thoughts shared throughout this text can serve as a *"roadmap"* to a better life.

## - Empowering Fundamentals -

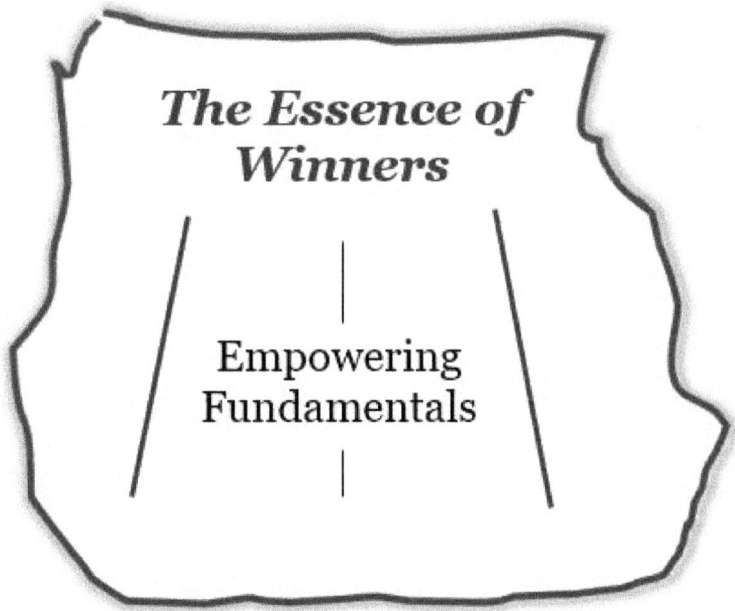

# The Essence of Winners

## Empowering Fundamentals

*"It is not the mountain we conquer,*

*but ourselves."*

*– Edmund Hillary*

# Self (Awareness)

> *"Knowing yourself is the beginning*
> *of all wisdom."*
> - Aristotle

Have you ever looked in the mirror and, while looking at your reflection, realized that the one peering out is distinct from the image being reflected? Hopefully, you have. If not, it is my sincere wish that you will have the experience.

For those who have, it is a surreal moment, a glimpse of our true essence, or "*self*," an awakened instance, if you will.

At this moment, one might note changes in stature, weight, hair—thinning or greying—and skin tone and rigidity—wrinkled, stretched, or loose. The older we grow, the more apparent these changes become. Many of us are concerned, alarmed, or even shocked by our physical changes, so much so that we resort to all types of diets, exercises, wonder supplements, medicines, and surgical procedures to recover our youth.

It is like our body is our car, and our consciousness has discovered its frailties.

The Essence of Winners – *Self (Awareness)*

Whether we are aware or not, the source, energy, and conscience peeking through and operating our body is timeless, ageless, and boundless— *the real you.* More importantly, this unblemished, omnipotent presence has always been and is at our beck and call for our guidance and empowerment, but only as we become quiet, aware, and present; for many of us, a considerable undertaking as we are predominantly preoccupied with fending for today.

> Luckily for us, amid our daily lives, we can empower our lives by cultivating the power of "*self-awareness,*" being conscious of how you perceive yourself; that is *Internal self-awareness,* which is understanding your thoughts, values, beliefs, emotions, feelings, motivations, and behaviors, and *external self-awareness,* which is understanding how others see you and the impact of your behavior on them.[1]

Self (Awareness) will lead to emotional and personal growth and improved relationships. With your profound understanding of self, you become the master of your journey and develop a firm grasp of your personality, strengths, and weaknesses.

*When not rooted in*
*authentic self and awareness,*
*one can easily become*
*a victim of*
*compromising thoughts*
*and exposures.*
- HCJ

## *A Zen Parable on Self-Awareness*

A tough, brawny samurai once approached a Zen master who was deep in meditation.

Impatient and discourteous, the samurai demanded in his husky voice so accustomed to forceful yelling, *"Tell me the nature of heaven and hell."*

The Zen master opened his eyes, looked the samurai in the face, and replied with a certain scorn, "Why should I answer to a shabby, disgusting, despondent slob like you? A worm like you, do you think I should tell you anything? I can't stand you. Get out of my sight. I have no time for silly questions."

The samurai could not bear these insults. *Consumed by rage*, he drew his sword and raised it to sever the master's head at once.

Looking straight into the samurai's eyes, the Zen master tenderly declared, *"That's hell."*

The samurai froze. He immediately understood that anger had him in its grip. His mind had just created his own hell—one filled with resentment, hatred, self-defense, and fury. He realized that he was so deep in his torment that he was ready to kill somebody. The samurai's eyes filled with tears. Setting his sword aside, he put his palms together and obsequiously bowed in gratitude for this insight.

The Zen master gently acknowledged with a delicate smile, *"And that's heaven."*

https://www.linkedin.com/pulse/power-self-awareness-discovering-your-true-self-myllama/

**Things to ponder**

The Zen "Parable on Self-Awareness" shares that heaven and hell are states of mind. Heaven represents a positive, life-affirming consciousness, and hell is our negative, reactionary mind, often resulting from our convoluted, perplexed thoughts. And that we live our best lives with calm, discerning, instructed minds.

Ultimately, *"self-awareness"* is a psychological state in which our inner person becomes the focus of attention, not as a narcissist who only cares about him or herself, but a reflective, conscious being empowering their and everyone else's lives. A mental and physical reference point in which one is in harmonious balance with one's thoughts, feelings, emotions, words, behaviors, actions, and reactions.

This is what the content of these writings is about. Our reacquaintance with our innate might—our intellectual, emotional, and spiritual grandness—our willingness to become mindful, cognizant, and proactive to shake free of our lives' detrimental thoughts and turmoil and enjoy inspiring wellness and success.

Am I self-aware?

If "no," why not?

How can I benefit from becoming more self-aware?

"Watch your thoughts,
they become your words.
• • •
Watch your words,
they become your actions.
• • •
Watch your actions,
they become your habits.
• • •
Watch your habits,
they become your character.
• • •
Watch your character,
it becomes your destiny."
- Anonymous

# Desire & Intention

> *"You are what your deepest desire is.*
> *As is your desire, so is your intention.*
> *As is your intention, so is your will.*
> *As is your will, so is your deed.*
> *As is your deed, so is your destiny."*
> — *Upanishads*

Our lives are driven by thoughts and words which embody their meaning. And although all thoughts arise from within, they are often triggered by the environment we partake in. Dr. Fred Luskin at Stanford University states that the average person has over 60,000 thoughts a day, 90 % being repetitive from the day and previous days.

Generally speaking, we have positive and negative thoughts related to love, joy, sadness, contentment, anger, desire, intention, etc. Similar to our lives, for the launching point of these writings, we begin by focusing on *"desire and intention"* as they are the precursors and impetus for achievement and the topics that follow.

*Desire* can arise from conceptual thoughts, like a wish, or physical needs, like thirst or hunger. On the other hand, *intention* is usually seen as an affirming, intensifying accelerant; what we put our undivided attention on tends to grow. Either way, being closely related but still distinct concepts, it is akin to what came first, the chicken or the egg, and at least one must be present to fuel our fire.

As per Dictionary.com and AI, *desire* is to want or long for. It's often tied to emotions and can be inspired by personal needs or aspirations. For instance, you might desire success, love, or adventure.

*Intention* is the act or instance of determining mentally upon some action or result. It is more about purpose and direction. It involves making a *conscious decision* to achieve a specific outcome. *While desire can be about what you want, intention is about the actions you commit to in order to attain those desires.*

In many ways, intention can help channel and manifest your desires into reality. By setting clear intentions, you can create a roadmap that guides your actions toward fulfilling what you truly want.[1]

*"Learn to harness the power of intention, and you can create anything you desire."*

- Deepak Chopra

# Mastering Desire, Will and Intention

## What is Creative Manifestation?

We are creators, and that means we are more than people- artists, writers, teachers, carpenters, welders, electricians, doctors, lawyers, parents, children, etc. We co-create our experience through our thoughts, our words, our deeds, and our will. Everything we do is a creative act. So our choice becomes do we do this consciously or based on habit and previous programming?

### Components of Manifestation

There are three key components to creative manifestation:

### Desire

From a mindfulness perspective, there are two distinct types of desire. *The first is the desire of a wanting mind.* It is a thirst that feels it can only be satisfied by something outside of the self. In Buddhism, this would be one of the mind poisons. It is this type of desire that keeps you stuck in the cycle of birth-death and re-birth. This craving is looking to be satisfied, we partake in the desire, we feel a brief sense of satiety and then we repeat the cycle over again.

*The second type of desire is the desire to do.* This is our want to be connected to something bigger than ourselves. It is about bringing what is within ourselves into the outer world. There is a palpable sense of energy and inspiration about participating in a way that creates something meaningful. *Desire is the driving force behind our actions, so the question becomes, does the wanting come from a place of lack, or does it come from a place of adding meaning?*

## Will

Will is a bit harder to define, but it is the power source composed of two distinct characteristics. It is emotion, aka the desire coupled with conscious choice. So, the desire to do, added to the power of choice, gives us will.

## Intention

*Our intention is the container for our will and desire.* The ultimate ideal or the big picture of what it is we want to see come to fruition. It is a single word or phrase that unifies the desire, choice, and deed.

## How to Create What We Desire?

By combining all of the above components, we can co-create our world. We need to understand the story around our desire. Why do we want what we want? Does it come from the desire to do or the desire to satisfy? Once we understand our story, we develop meaning.

When something becomes meaningful to us, i.e., we understand how it fits our worldview and value system, then we make choices in alignment with them. This is an expression of our will. If all of this is done with a *unifying intention* and we are consistent in the expression of our desires, will, deeds, and intention – we consciously co-create our reality.

https://chaosandlight.com/desire-will-intention/
angela@chaosandlight.com

## Things to Ponder

As we understand the role that *"desire and intention"* play as the incipient catalyst of our lives, we realize that these thoughts are the tip of the iceberg, the *prelude* to manifesting our short and long-term achievements and success, and the need to empower our birthing thoughts to fruition with the additional thoughts, words, and actions that follow.

How do I see the interplay between my desires and intentions?

Do I accomplish what I set out to do?

# Motivation & Discipline

*"Motivation is the impetus for what you are capable of doing, and discipline is how you accomplish it."*

*- HCJ*

In life, being motivated and disciplined are key factors to having a successful journey.

A healthy balance of *"motivation"* and discipline is essential for personal fulfillment and happiness. Success is not a by-product of osmosis. Motivation must be tempered with discipline, as most thoughts and actions by themselves tend to fizzle out.

By the same token, discipline without motivation is tantamount to stalemate. The trick, then, is how we foster and combine motivation, incentives, and reasons to act with long-term engagement and discipline.

For successful individuals, this is pretty much a given. They know that accomplishment, achievement, and prosperity require inspiration, commitment, action, and discipline.

But for many, this is a struggle. They make their way through life unmotivated and uncommitted, living a substandard life, never fulfilling their potential, and sometimes blaming others or life circumstances for their lack of happiness or success.

For those who struggle with motivation and discipline it's never too late to learn and apply these tenets of success to your lives. The only thing required is the desire, willingness, and commitment to learn, explore, and follow through.

Steps towards finding, applying, and maintaining *motivation* are setting clear goals and a clear direction and breaking goals into smaller, manageable tasks. Visualize success to maintain focus and motivation. Find your why; understand why you want to achieve your goals.

Connecting your goals to your values and passions can provide a strong sense of purpose and motivation. Surround yourself with supportive people who inspire and encourage you. Also, organize your physical and digital spaces to minimize distractions and promote productivity.

Acknowledge and celebrate your achievements, no matter how small. Recognizing your progress can boost your confidence and motivation to keep going. Be willing to adapt and adjust your plans as needed.

Flexibility can help you navigate challenges and setbacks without losing motivation. Prioritize self-care activities such as exercise, proper nutrition, adequate sleep, and relaxation. A healthy body and mind are essential for sustained motivation.

Surround yourself with sources of inspiration, whether through books, podcasts, videos, or connecting with people who have achieved similar goals. Focus on the positive aspects of your journey and maintain a hopeful outlook, even in the face of challenges.

Optimism can fuel your motivation and help you overcome obstacles. Remember that motivation can fluctuate, and it's normal to experience ups and downs. The key is staying committed to your goals and taking small steps forward, even when motivation is low.[1]

*"Today is*

*your opportunity to*

*build the tomorrow you want."*

- Ken Poirot

## *Tony Robbins*

Tony Robbins (Anthony Jay Robbins), as a man, is a walking inspiration. He came from an extremely abusive household in his childhood, with a mother who was chronically addicted to drugs and alcohol and would often abuse Tony and his siblings mentally, verbally, and physically until one day, Tony abandoned it all and sought to tell his story.

He eventually would become a world-renowned public speaker and life coach, having investments in over 30 companies and being known for his works on books and charitable organizations that have provided millions without food with meals.

As stated previously, Tony had grown up in a house in turmoil. His mother was dangerously addicted to both drugs and alcohol and would often turn to Tony and his siblings to relieve her hatred upon them.

There are stories from Tony's childhood where he mentions a time when his mother had poured a bottle of liquid soap into his mouth and forced him to swallow it. Despite the torture that Tony had to endure mentally and physically, he always looked out for his siblings as the eldest of the lot.

His abusive mother would remarry four times during Tony's childhood, further meaning that he and his siblings were left to fend for themselves, with Tony assuming that role of responsibility to ensure that he could relieve his siblings of the life they, too had to endure as much as he possibly could.

Eventually, the time would come for Tony to leave home following an incident where his own mother had chased after him with a knife, forcing him out of the home in fear for his own life. This was the straw that broke the camel's back, and Tony never returned home from that day onwards; however, he would continue to support his siblings who remained trapped in the hell that was his mother's home despite his low-income jobs and living day to day.

Tony had much to be proud of even at this stage of his life with the resolve he had shown to endure the years of abuse his mother had thrown at him, as well as the responsibility and courage to stand up for his siblings and support them in their time of need.

However, greater things were on the horizon for Tony when he decided to take a chance in contacting famous motivational speaker Jim Rohn. Jim would become inspired by Tony's story and lead him to a life of telling his story and helping others. Tony would go on to travel around his nation, spreading the consistent message that your past does not lead to your future.

His first book 'Unlimited Power' exploded him onto the scene, leading him to where he is now in life, having investments in over 30 companies, as well as being worth in excess of 500 million, along with him following his initial morals of helping those in need that he had taken from his childhood, with his charity now having fed over 50million people across the globe.

Tony's story has certainly changed his life, and in almost every way, for the better.

## What lessons can we learn from Tony Robbin's Life?

### Your Past Will Never Define Your Future

One message that anybody can take away from Tony's life story is that of a message that Tony preaches himself that your past will never define who you can become in your future. Tony's story is a perfect example of someone overcoming the most immense of traumas in life to become someone who excelled in every area he touched.

He has achieved the unimaginable and is now in a position where he not only has helped himself but continues to help millions of others around the world. He did not allow his past to define his future, and neither should you. That is the lesson.

## *Assume Responsibility for Those in Need*

Despite Tony undoubtedly struggling with his own demons throughout his childhood and most likely continuing into his adulthood, he always sought to help those in need, starting with his siblings. Despite Tony having to endure the bulk of the torture at home, he still always put his younger siblings at the top of his priorities when seeking to make sure that they get out of the abusive household that they had unfortunately grown up in, continuing to do so even when he was living day to day on little money away from them.

His responsibility and tack for assisting those in need continued into his current life, with his charitable work and assistance of those who come from similar or not so similar backgrounds to himself showing that Tony has achieved his life goal of assuming responsibility for others in their time of need.

In conclusion, Tony's life is one that no child should have to go through; however, unfortunately, millions do. He shows a light to these people that there is light at the end of the tunnel and that anything is possible so long as you manage to find a way to escape the shackles placed on you by the issues you are facing, and to face the demons in your life. His story is one of inspiration and passion and his life is one that we could all learn from in some way or another.

https://suninme.org/true-story/tony-robbinshttps://suninme.org/true-story/tony-robbins Nathan Brennan

**Things to Ponder!**


Like all thoughts and actions, *"motivation"* is either self-generated or the result of lived circumstances. As per the story "Tony Robbins," most of us will experience difficulties throughout our lives. But we cannot let onerous circumstances negatively impact our lives. Tony's success is an inspiration for all to draw from and a gleaming example of someone who, despite his ordeals, motivates himself and others daily to succeed.


Am I self-motivated?

    If "yes," how?

    If "not," why not?

Do I let current or past difficulties stifle my motivation?

    If "yes," how or why?

    If "yes," how do I change this?

# Discipline

*"For whatever goal you want to achieve,*
*there is discomfort along that path.*
*Self-discipline drives you through*
*this discomfort and allows*
*you to achieve and attain.*
*It's an essential component of mastery,*
*and nothing great was ever*
*accomplished without it."*
*- Peter Hollins*

"*Discipline*" is the common denominator for achievement. But, like all else, it cannot exist by itself. It needs motivation to kick start it, as well as to provide continuous fuel. Together, discipline and motivation form an intricate catalyst to attaining our goals and living rewarding, gratifying lives.

Along with its dose, steady allotment of motivation, among the qualities necessary for cultivating a disciplined life are self-control, developing habits, and defining and pursuing goals—conforming and consistently applying well-defined rules, practices, and drills.

Anyone can cultivate a culture of discipline. It is simply a matter of deciding if your priority in life is to be the best you can be, not only for yourself but also for your family, friends, and community.

Additional traits that disciplined people have in common are consistency and adherence to principles; they are true to their word, avoid temptation, take care of themselves, set boundaries, revel in routine, and lead with their minds instead of their moods.[1]

*"Motivation gets you going, but discipline keeps you growing."*

*- John C. Maxwell*

# *Self-discipline Changed My Life*

Up until my freshman year of college, I practiced little to no self-discipline. It's not that I purposely avoided it, I just simply didn't care about it. Nor was I aware of how important self-discipline is to a person's character, well-being, and overall quality of life.

Self-discipline is about consistency. Ironically, often times it is hard to be consistent. I found this happened to me during my time of becoming self-disciplined. I was either going at it 100% or 0%.

When I was a sophomore in college, I stumbled upon a book called "Becoming Human" by Jean Vanier. It had a dramatic impact on my life and, oddly enough, made me much more self-aware. I had always considered myself a self-aware person, but I was never self-disciplined.

This new knowledge triggered a dramatic change in my life. I started waking up at the same time every day and began each day with yoga and a devotional study. I would drink the same tea and leave my home at the same time every day. I would work out at the same time everyday, run the same amount of miles, and go to bed at 11 pm every night.

For me, it's taken time to come to a healthy level of self-discipline. To stay balanced, but also allow for schedule changes and regime changes that are often times unpredictable.

Learning healthy self-discipline has truly made me a more organized person while also allowing space to be more efficient and productive overall. Self-discipline is all about the mind. It can turn you into a healthier person, a stronger individual, and even make you a morning-loving person. Self-discipline brings consistency and balance to the crazy and unpredictable world we live in.

https://www.quora.com/How-has-self-discipline-changed-your-life-Share-some-inspiring-stories Lindsay Fuce

**Things to Ponder!**

As shared in "Self-discipline Changed My Life," nothing of lasting value, well-being, or quality of life is possible without *"self-discipline."* It is the common denominator for a successful, empowered, balanced, happy life.

Am I a disciplined person?

If "yes," how?

If not, what prevents me from living a disciplined life?

*"Discipline is the bridge between goals and accomplishments."*

*- Jim Rohn*

# *Willpower and Discipline*

*Vanderlei Cordeiro de Lima* was the leading runner in the 2004 Summer Olympics marathon. At his pace, he was sure to win first place and secure the gold medal which would've brought pride and glory to his family and country.

Near the end of the marathon, he was *attacked* by a spectator. The spectator actually sidelined into him. Intentionally. In public.

That brief, 10-second-long distraction was enough to completely disrupt De Lima's mental AND physical rhythm, both of which are critical to running long-distance marathons. He was quickly surpassed by two other runners and was evidently off his game for the remainder of the marathon. He finished in third place in surprisingly good spirits and received the bronze medal.

*What people remember is that he crossed the finish line with a smile despite what had happened to him just moments before. This was a man who was robbed of first place and an Olympic gold medal in a matter of seconds.*

Imagine training for something your entire life and being so close to accomplishing something extraordinary. Something that brings you, your family, and your country great pride and happiness and puts you in the history books.

Only to be robbed in a matter of seconds in the most outrageous and nonsensical way possible. By something that should never have happened in the first place.

De Lima could've stopped running when that incident happened. He could've attacked the trespasser. He could've complained endlessly to the officials. But he pushed past, he ran, and he finished.

Even after the fiasco, words like "furious" or "hatred" were evidently not in De Lima's vocabulary. Holding a relentless vendetta against his perpetrator was clearly not important to him.

Even when a fellow Olympian earnestly offered his own gold medal to De Lima, De Lima responded, "*I am happy with mine - it is bronze but means gold.*"

De Lima went on to win a variety of awards commemorating his self-discipline and spirit of sportsmanship. He also went on to light the cauldron at the 2016 Rio Olympics. It takes immense willpower and discipline to run and finish as a top contender for a marathon in the Olympics, but I think what makes

De Lima so special is his willpower and discipline to look past something so *ill-fated* and still come out on top. He truly lives a life of no regrets.

And I don't remember who won first or second place in that 2004 Summer Olympics Marathon. But I remember Vanderlei Cordeiro de Lima. *The man is a legend.*

https://www.quora.com/How-has-self-discipline-changed-your-life-Share-some-inspiring-stories Kevin E. Luo

**Things to Ponder!**

*"Disciplined"* individuals are well aware of the fruits of their and others' hard work. Therefore, they are usually honorable beings living by a high code of ethics, as demonstrated in "Willpower and Discipline."

As this story exemplifies, success requires self-discipline, effort, consistency, and sometimes luck. It is not a search or application of a quick solution, as these have no lasting value.

How can I be more disciplined?

# Perseverance & Resilience

Like two sides of a coin, *"perseverance and resilience"* are essential for success. They are the acts of purposefully, with steadfast and unwavering resolution, applying yourself to a task, undertaking, or project regardless of the duration required to reach a desired result.

It is pursuing and achieving something difficult despite experiencing opposition, challenges, obstacles, uncertainty, adversity, failure, pain, or heartache. The very application of perseverance strengthens our determination, builds our resiliency, cultivates our patience, and is a cornerstone parameter to all successful life endeavors.[1]

We will often be confronted with an arduous situation, problem, job, or even adverse health issue that we must traverse. Usually, the difference between victoriously navigating the circumstance or failing is as simple as instructing yourself and applying your undivided attention to the matter at hand.

The Essence of Winners – *Perseverance & Resilience*

Some mistakingly choose or believe it's much easier to disregard or ignore a difficult predicament than to apply their energy and mental fortitude and persevere to a fruitful result. There are no *freebies* in life. We either choose to win or lose by default.

Much like everything that leads to success, practice is required to develop the skills of perseverance and resilience. With diligence, one learns to zero in on solutions instead of problems and not give up or abandon a situation. The focus is on the overall picture, its completion or attainment.

"The only guarantee for failure is to stop trying."

- Unknown

# *Chair the Hope*

In 2001, Nathan Ogden raced down an Oregon ski slope, launching himself off a jump over 30 feet into the air. While he had done this many times, something was different on this day. He caught more air than he intended to, which rotated his body backward, slamming him onto the slope.

He tried to stand, but his legs wouldn't move. He soon learned that his neck had shattered.

Over the next few months, this married father of two threw his heart and soul into rehab and remained confident that he would walk again, despite what the doctors said. Gradually, as he gained sensation in his legs and a little independence, his doctors called his progress *miraculous*. But he wanted his health to progress faster.

He worked tirelessly to regain use of his upper body, and while he could hardly move his legs, he was convinced that one day he would walk again.

He eventually regained 50% of his body movement, but more trouble was yet to come. In 2003, just 13 months after his skiing accident, Ogden caught pneumonia and fell unconscious in his sleep.

When his wife couldn't wake him, he was rushed to the ER, where technicians accidentally dropped him to the floor while x-raying his lungs.

For the second time, Ogden had broken his neck. But this time, the break was higher up, which permanently paralyzed him. All of his hard work and hundreds of hours of rehab crashed to the floor. Years later, he now has very little control of his upper body and no sensation from his chest down.

But when asked what went through his mind when he woke up and learned his neck was broken again, he said, *The first words I said to my wife when she told me were, bring it on. I knew that if I had done it once, I could do it again.*

Ogden tried to be positive throughout the coming years but says that was easier said than done. He had fought so hard to progress after his first accident, only to have it ripped out from under him.

Ogden felt trapped, noting *I lost my job, friends, self-esteem, and almost my marriage. Being physically paralyzed is extremely difficult, but not moving mentally is painfully worse.*

But with his positive attitude, Ogden learned to feel more compassion and empathy towards others than he'd ever experienced. He believes he went through his challenges in order to magnify the positive results.

He continues to fight a daily battle against adversity, and since his second paralysis, he has been skydiving, gone river rafting, hunting, snow skiing, water skiing and even completed a half-triathlon.

He is even venturing into consulting, public speaking, and writing a book to inspire as many as possible to believe in hope and progress.

Ogden notes that while he may not be able to move his legs or walk, he can stand up and face his fears, and he seeks to convince other people that they can, too.

https://www.developgoodhabits.com/perseverance-stories-cm1/ June 8, 2023 Connie Stemmle

## Things to Ponder!

While most likely we will never experience such a fate, Nathan's indomitable spirit allows him to live a fulfilling life. It also puts into perspective that most of our challenges are trivial compared to his.

For many, self-doubt is one of the biggest obstacles to success. But as "Chair the Hope" exemplifies, just because one faces difficulties, one should not stop, take the easy way out, or give up on our dreams.

Success doesn't come easily or quickly at any stage, and countless hurdles must be cleared before reaching one's goals. The key that separates success from disappointment is *"persistence, resilience,"* and realizing that obstacles and failure are integral to achieving.

Remember, you will experience both good and bad, positive and negative situations throughout life. To persevere and live a rewarding, healthier, and happier life, we must learn from the harsh and focus on the positives as life goes on, no matter what.

Franklin D. Roosevelt served three terms as the president of The United States despite having polio and being confined to leg braces and a wheelchair.

Nelson Mandela spent twenty-seven years in prison for his commitment to anti-apartheid and conviction to justice and equality before being freed and becoming the democratically elected President of South Africa.

The Essence of Winners – *Perseverance & Resilience*

Mahatma Gandhi's philosophical and persistent stance of non-violent descent led his country to freedom from British colonial rule.

*Remember, winners never quit, and quitters never win!*

Am I persistent and resilient?

 If "no," why not?

 Does this prevent me from achieving?

# Adversity & Change

People shunt adversity like a harmful plague. This non-welcoming behavior is usually learned from our parents, culture, society, and even past personal hardship. But truth be told, without difficulty in our lives, there is little emotional, psychological, or character growth.

Hard times, distress, suffering, and misfortunes are catalysts for personal development. Like the clam whose grain of sand so irritated its existence that it developed a beautiful pearl, so too can adversity help us become stronger.

"_Adversity_" is a challenging circumstance, event, situation, misfortune, or calamity that an individual or group may face. It can disrupt one's health, financial security, profession, job, and personal and social relationships. It can be transformative, pushing people to develop coping skills, increase strength, and grow.[1]

The question is how do we change our understanding, effectively cope with, and even embrace, the harsh, the difficult, the unsettling, and demanding?

A simple answer is to learn from and emulate the response and behavior of successful individuals who deal with tough times and stressful events. It is not that they are immune to it.

It's that they know that most troublesome times, circumstances, and situations are there for their growth and that maintaining an open nature, learning patience, allotting time, persevering, and educating oneself are essential for overcoming.

*"It's your reaction
to adversity, not adversity itself,
that determines how your life's
story will develop."*

*- Dieter F. Uchtdorf*

## *Potatoes, Eggs, and Coffee Beans*

Once upon a time, a daughter complained to her father that her life was miserable and that she didn't know how she would make it. She was tired of fighting and struggling all the time. It seemed that just as one problem was solved, another soon followed.

Her father, a chef, took her to the kitchen. He filled three pots with water and placed each on a high fire. Once the three pots began to boil, he placed potatoes in one pot, eggs in the second pot, and ground coffee beans in the third pot.

He then let them sit and boil without saying a word to his daughter. The daughter moaned and impatiently waited, wondering what he was doing.

After twenty minutes, he turned off the burners. He took the potatoes from the pot and placed them in a bowl. He pulled the eggs out and placed them in a bowl.

He then ladled the coffee out and placed it in a cup. Turning to her, he asked. "Daughter, what do you see?"

"Potatoes, eggs, and coffee," she hastily replied.

"Look closer," he said, "and touch the potatoes." She did and noted that they were soft. He then asked her to take an egg and break it. After pulling off the shell, she observed the hard-boiled egg. Finally, he asked her to sip the coffee. Its rich aroma brought a smile to her face.

"Father, what does this mean?" she asked.

*He then explained that the potatoes, the eggs, and the coffee beans had each faced the same adversity– the boiling water.*

*However, each one reacted differently.*

The potato went in strong, hard, and unrelenting, but in boiling water, it became soft and weak.

The egg was fragile, with the thin outer shell protecting its liquid interior until it was put in the boiling water. Then, the inside of the egg became hard.

However, the ground coffee beans were unique. After they were exposed to the boiling water, they changed the water and created something new.

*"Which are you,"* he asked his daughter. "When adversity knocks on your door, how do you respond? "Are you a potato, an egg, or a coffee bean?" Moral: *In*

*life, things happen around us, things happen to us, but the only thing that truly matters is what happens within us.*

https://www.4recruitmentservices.com/blog/2017/08/15-motivational-and-inspiring-short-stories?source=google.com

## Things to Ponder!

As "Potatoes, Eggs, and Coffee Beans" shares with us, all of us will experience our share of *"adversity,"* suffering, pain, misery, sweat, and discomfort. But how we perceive and react to life's hardships, calamities, and misfortunes dictates our response and attitude towards life.

Being wheelchair-bound for over fifty years has brought to light that no matter the difficulty or challenge, I choose to learn, confront where need be, overcome when possible, and make the best of any situation. Why should we make the journey more stressful or disturbing by responding negatively?

How can I change my perception or reaction to adversity?

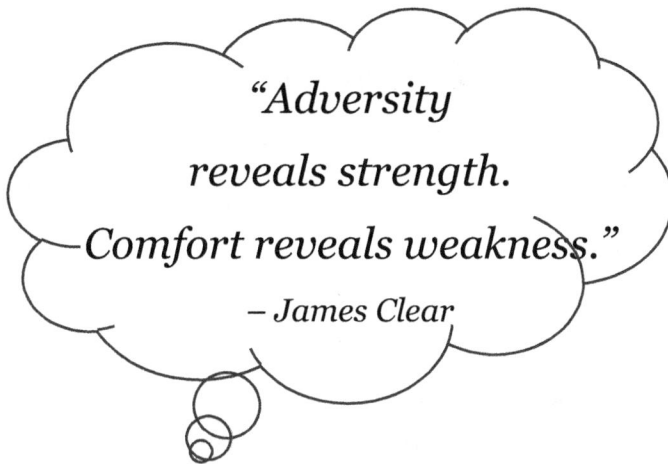

"Adversity
reveals strength.
Comfort reveals weakness."
– James Clear

## *The Potter and The Clay*

The story is told of a couple who went to England to celebrate their 25th wedding anniversary and shopped at a beautiful antique store. They both liked antiques, pottery, and especially teacups, so when spotting an exceptional cup, they asked, *"May we see that? We've never seen a cup quite so beautiful."*

As the lady handed it to them, suddenly, the teacup spoke, *"You don't understand.* It said *I have not always been a tea cup. There was a time when I was just a lump of red clay. My master took me and rolled me, pounded and patted me over and over, and I yelled out, Don't do that. I don't like it! Let me alone, but he only smiled and gently said;* Not yet!"

*"Then, WHAM! I was placed on a spinning wheel, and suddenly, I was spun around and around and around. Stop it! I'm getting so dizzy! I'm going to be sick! I screamed."* But the master only nodded and said quietly; Not yet.

He spun me and poked and prodded and bent me out of shape to suit himself, and then, he put me in the oven. I never felt such heat. I yelled and knocked and pounded at the door. *"Help! Get me out of here!"* Not yet. When I thought I couldn't bear it another minute, the door opened. He carefully took me out and put me on the shelf, and I began to cool.

"Oh, that felt so good! *Ah, this is much better,*" I thought. But, after I cooled, he picked me up and brushed and painted me all over. The fumes were horrible, "*Oh, please, Stop it! Stop it!*" I cried. He only shook his head and said. Not yet.

Then suddenly, he put me back into the oven. Only it was not like the first time. This time, it was twice as hot, and I just knew I would suffocate.

"*I begged, I pleaded, I screamed, I cried,*" I was convinced I would never make it. I was ready to give up, and just then, the door opened. And he took me out and again placed me on the shelf, where I cooled and waited and waited, wondering, "*What's he going to do to me next?*"

An hour later, he handed me a mirror and said, "*Look at yourself.*" And I did. I said, "*That's not me. That couldn't be me. It's beautiful. I'm beautiful!*"

Quietly, he spoke: "*Iwant you to remember;* then, he said, *I know it hurt to be rolled and pounded and patted, but had I just left you alone, you'd have dried up. I know it made you dizzy to spin around on the*

65

*wheel, but if I had stopped, you would have crumbled." "I know it hurt, and it was hot and disagreeable in the oven, but if I hadn't put you there, you would have cracked. I know the fumes were bad when I brushed and painted you all over, but if I hadn't done that, you never would have hardened. You would not have had any color in your life."*

*"And if I hadn't put you back in that second oven, you wouldn't have survived for long because the hardness would not have held. Now, you are a finished product. Now, you are what I had in mind when I first began with you."*

https://paterallen2.wordpress.com/2016/08/09/insightstwo-inspiring-stories-the-potter-and-the-clay-building-bridges/ Author Unknown

## Things to Ponder!

We are all a work in progress. "The Potter and The Clay" points out that *"adversity"* can be emotional and physical. And though not consistently recognized, it usually serves to make one stronger.

How do I view or react when confronted with adversity? Can I derive benefit and growth from my hardships?

# Change

> *"The key to change... is to let go of fear."*
> – Rosanne Cash

*"Change"* is life's catalyst and only constant. Yet many are conflicted by it, are adverse to it, or downright fear it. Where did we learn to view change as an unfavorable thing?

Throughout life, we will all experience good, positive, rewarding change. We are not even aware of some of it, as if our bodies were not in perpetual cellular replacement, in which every seven to ten years we are made anew, we would cease to exist.

But it is usually the fearful, problematic, troublesome, or painful exposures that we run from. Yet, more often than not, life's most rewarding teachings come from there.

Now, do we allow harsh times and change to impact our present and future response and understanding negatively, or do we step back, assess, learn, adapt, and embrace the situation for what it is worth?

The power of winners and successful individuals is *directly linked* to how well they embrace change, pivot, traverse difficulties, trials, and tribulations, and use these to empower their beings and goals. After all, there is usually a beautiful rainbow after every rainstorm.

*"Change the way*
*you look at things, and*
*the things you look at change."*
*- Wayne W. Dyer*

## *Shark Bait*

During a research experiment, a marine biologist placed a shark into a large holding tank and then released several small bait fish into the tank.

As you would expect, the shark quickly swam around the tank, attacked, and ate the smaller fish.

The marine biologist then inserted a strong piece of clear fiberglass into the tank, creating two separate partitions. She then put the shark on one side of the fiberglass and a new set of bait fish on the other.

Again, the shark quickly attacked. This time, however, the shark slammed into the fiberglass divider and bounced off. Undeterred, the shark kept repeating this behavior every few minutes to no avail. Meanwhile, the bait fish swam around unharmed in the second partition. Eventually, about an hour into the experiment, the shark gave up.

This experiment was repeated several dozen times over the next few weeks. Each time, the shark got less aggressive and made fewer attempts to attack the bait fish until, eventually, the shark got tired of hitting the fiberglass divider and simply stopped attacking altogether.

The marine biologist then removed the fiberglass divider, but the shark didn't attack. The shark was trained to believe a barrier existed between it and the bait fish, so the bait fish swam wherever they wished, free from harm.

https://www.marcandangel.com/2013/05/21/4-short-stories-change-the-way-you-think/ - The Road Less Traveled

## Things to Ponder!

After experiencing setbacks and failures, many of us emotionally give up and stop trying. Like the shark in the story, we assume or believe that *"change"* is impossible and that we will fail with new attempts or circumstances because of unsuccessful past experiences.

We continue to see barriers in our heads, even though, more often than not, no 'real' barrier exists between where we are and where we want to go.

Am I open to change? If "yes," how?
Do I dislike "change?" If "yes," why?
　　How can I learn to embrace it?

*"Be the change
that you wish to see in
the world."*

*– Mahatma Gandhi*

## *All the Difference in The World*

Every Sunday morning, I take a light jog around a park near my home. There's a lake located in one corner of the park. Each time I jog by this lake, I see the same elderly woman sitting at the water's edge with a small metal cage sitting beside her.

This past Sunday, my curiosity got the best of me, so I stopped jogging and walked over to her. As I got closer, I realized that the metal cage was, in fact, a small trap. There were three turtles, unharmed, slowly walking around the base of the trap. She had a fourth turtle in her lap that she was carefully scrubbing with a spongy brush.

*"Hello,"* I said. *"I see you here every Sunday morning. If you don't mind my nosiness, I'd love to know what you're doing with these turtles."*

She smiled. *"I'm cleaning off their shells,* she replied. *Anything on a turtle's shell, like algae or scum, reduces the turtle's ability to absorb heat and impedes its ability to swim. It can also corrode and weaken the shell over time."*

*"Wow! That's really nice of you!"* I exclaimed.

She went on: *"I spend a couple of hours each Sunday morning relaxing by this lake and helping these little guys out. It's my own strange way of making a difference."*

"But don't most freshwater turtles live their whole lives with algae and scum hanging from their shells?" I asked.

*"Yep, sadly, they do,"* she replied.

I scratched my head.

*"Well then, don't you think your time could be better spent? I mean, I think your efforts are kind and all, but there are freshwater turtles living in lakes all around the world. And 99% of these turtles don't have kind people like you to help them clean off their shells. So, no offense, but how exactly are your localized efforts here truly making a difference?"*

The woman giggled aloud. She then looked down at the turtle in her lap, scrubbed off the last piece of algae from its shell, and said, *"Sweetie, if this little guy could talk, he'd tell you I just made all the difference in the world."*

https://www.marcandangel.com/2013/05/21/4-short-stories-change-the-way-you-think/

## Things to Ponder!

As the story denotes, at times, the significance of the agent *"change"* is not readily apparent to us. We look for grandiose gestures instead of seeing the invaluable in small deeds. One need not worry about changing the world. We only need to make a positive difference or deed to the people and things around us. This, in turn, will be reflected in the world. Wake up every morning and know that what you do makes a difference.

As Mother Teresa of Calcutta brilliantly said, *"Not all of us can do great things. But we can do small things with great love."*

How can I become more receptive to the force that is *change* and use it as a *stepping stone* that can provide me and others with opportunities for growth, empowerment, and success?

# Fear & Failure

*"Fear kills more dreams than failure ever will."*
- *Suzy Kassem*

Whether successful or not, throughout our lives, we will encounter situations and circumstances that will trigger *"fear"* within us. How do we respond? Do we flee or fight and overcome?

For most of us, fear is a learned behavioral response. *Personal fear of injury, ailment, emotional or physical pain, and death. Or social fear, the avoidance of negative judgment and rejection from others, and the inability to take care of, lead, or perform at home, school, or work.*

*Specifically, fear is an emotional and physiological response to a perceived rational or irrational threat or situation.* When faced with a triggering circumstance, fear evokes a series of physiological changes in the body, such as increased heart rate, adrenaline release, and heightened senses, preparing the individual to react.

Fear varies from person to person, and individuals may experience fear differently based on their beliefs, personal traits, and past experiences. It can have both positive and negative effects. In a positive sense, fear can motivate individuals to take necessary steps to avert undesirable results or situations, thus enhancing the possibility of favorable outcomes. However, excessive fear adversely impacts our quality of life by debilitating our being, paralyzing our response, or leading to anxiety disorders.

The acronym "f e a r," denoting *"false evidence appearing real,"* has been used to describe a fictitious, foreboding thought. Whether authentic or not, *one can effectively overcome and manage most rational or imaginary fears by understanding the underlying causes and learning means, mechanisms, or solutions that temper or nullify the emotional response*—empowering one to function to the best of one's potential.

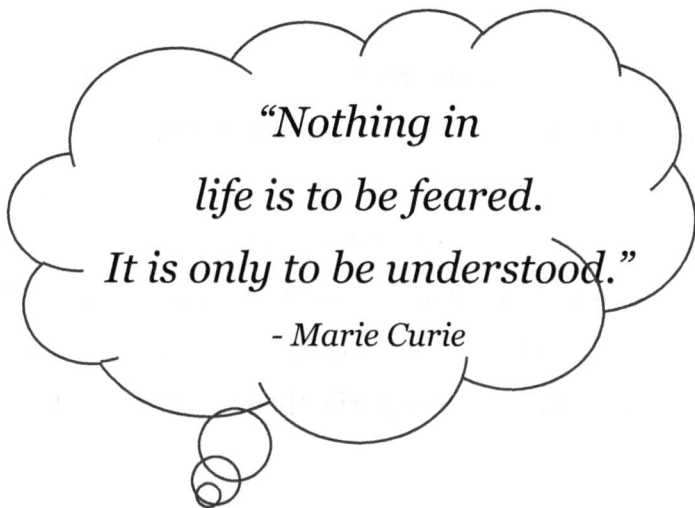

"Nothing in
life is to be feared.
It is only to be understood."
- Marie Curie

# Overcoming Fear

When people ask me what my biggest fears are, I usually give them the same answer: frogs, caves, and heights, in that order. It's an easy answer and a funny one—people always laugh at the frogs—but it's not the whole truth.

My father was mentally ill.

When I was a child, no one ever sat me down and explained to me what schizophrenia or bipolar disorder was. These were words I heard whispered in dark hallways. There was always an air of the clandestine about it, something to be kept hidden like my family were spies who'd mastered the subtle deception of appearing perfectly normal to the outside world.

No one else in my household had mental illness, so this was my first exposure to mental health as a shameful thing to be suffered alone.

*For a long time, my greatest fear was people finding out that my father had been so damaged that they would think I was damaged, too. In a way, it still kind of is.* When he put his arm through my bedroom window and severed his wrist down to the bone, I'm not sure if he was trying to kill himself, but he came very close. There's a scene in my latest book that echoes what it felt like to walk into my bedroom after that happened. There was blood on my carpet, blood on my toys, blood on my fairy quilt, blood on the walls in arcs, blood all over the kitchen where he'd stumbled after cutting himself.

Our neighbors saved him. They heard the crash, ran next door, and found him bleeding out. By that point, at 12 years old, I was thoroughly done. I remember being disappointed to find out that he was going to live.

I played Age of Empires on the computer at home instead of visiting him in the hospital. I didn't understand that he was sick. All I knew was he made my life hell.

Now that I'm older and understand that mental illness isn't something that people choose for themselves, I wish I'd had more compassion. More patience. More knowledge. I wonder if things could've ended differently for him if his illness had been treated with the same empathy that cancer patients are afforded.

My father isn't here anymore—his body remains, but his mind is gone, wiped by a stroke a few years ago. But still I wonder. I regret. I wish. I grieve. I forgive. I do these things every day.

I'm 27 now, and it's still hard. *Damn*, it is hard. A little part of me is still afraid that people are going to read this and think, *"How shameful to have had a father like that. To have that in your blood. If he was crazy, she must be, too."*

I fear my friends reading this. I fear my publishers reading this. I fear just about anyone reading this.

It's irrational and nonsensical, but it's true. Because as insidious as depression, anxiety, and mental illness are, so is the stigma that surrounds them. That's the fear I'm overcoming, slowly but surely. To be able to talk more openly about mental health and mental illness and the way it shapes so many of our lives. It should be normalized because it is normal.

*So this is me, facing my greatest fear right in front of you. How and when are you going to face yours?*

https://www.hellofears.com/stories/courage-is-speaking-openly-about-mental-illness Krystal Sutherland 27, California

**Things to Ponder!**

One of *"fear's"* weapons is its ability to spin false stories. It holds us back by creating compelling narratives in our heads that control our emotions, decisions, and actions.

The lack of knowledge, ignorance, assumptions, or our imagination often exaggerates our fears. They are accepted as true or sure to happen without proof.

Everyone in the world has fears that weaken their life. It's our *assignment* to conquer and rise above our fears. Like in the story "Overcoming Fear," you will find that many of our fears become more manageable and easier to deal with once informed on, confronted, or exposed. Some even dissolve.

Lastly, as per Zig Ziglar's definition of "fear," we can face everything and rise or forget everything and run. The choice is ours.

What are my fears?
Do they hold me back?
If "yes," how can I move past them?

# Failure

"*Failure only thrives as it's dealt within our mind.*"

*- HCJ*

"*Failure*" and fear are at times linked together as conjoined twins sharing a common skin. And even though we will be the recipients of both of these distressing conditions throughout our lives, it does not mean we must give up and throw in the towel.

To surpass failure, it helps to understand how, for most of us, our negative association with failure began. It did with our loved ones, friends, and society. Our parents, the very people who *encouraged us* to crawl, walk, and get educated so we could thrive in life, despite falling down an endless number of times and sometimes having to repeat emotional, intellectual, and educational setbacks, *simultaneously*, along with our friends and society were teaching us that *failure* was to be avoided at all cost.

Somewhere in life, they learned to see failure as harmful, and as they believed it would protect us from heartaches, struggles, and disappointments, they projected their belief and fear onto us.

But what is different about the understanding of failure by individuals like Thomas Edison, who invented the light bulb; Nikola Tesla, one of the fathers of modern electricity; the Wright brothers credited with man's first flight; Elan Musk, who most recently developed a reusable rocket, used to propel our spaceships into outer space, and returns and lands vertically on a pad and Michael Jordan which missed thousands of shots and lost many games, but whose persistence and dedication made him one of the greatest basketball players of all time.

The reality is that they, along with countless others, do not ascribe to, or are stopped by, the negative implications, complications, or suggestions of failure. For them, failure is seen and utilized as building blocks to success. They are lessons and opportunities to learn from. Hence, their understanding and interpretation of failure's role in our lives have provided humankind with incomparable progress.

Our common denominator with these men is that we are cloth from the same fabric regardless of our upbringing. To reach our potential, we must change our interpretation of failure, recognize our limitless nature, and understand that, more seldom than not, failures are our stepping stones to extraordinary results.

Per Dictionary.com and Chat GPT, *failure* is being unsuccessful in life's endeavors. It is difficult and painful, happens to all of us, and offers opportunities for growth. Dealing with and overcoming failure requires intellectual and emotional acceptance, reflecting, and analyzing its reasons to learn and grow. It requires setting small achievable goals, cultivating resilience, seeking support, taking action, including making changes and implementing the lessons learned, remaining positive, and celebrating the small wins along the way. [1]

*"Failure is
success in progress."*
*- Albert Einstein*

## *Ludwig van Beethoven*

### *(December 1770 – March 26, 1827)*

Ludwig van Beethoven is one of the most known classical composers of all time.

Beethoven's career as a composer did not start very well. His music teacher had said that "as a composer, he is hopeless". At a later stage in life, he was also strongly criticized for the music that he created. Yet, he became one of the biggest influencers who shifted the classical era towards the romantic era.

Although Beethoven is today known for his beautiful music, it did not come easily for him. Writing a symphony is a task that most of us can't even imagine. But to make it even worse, in his late 20's, Beethoven began to lose his hearing. And as years passed by, it only got worse.

It is said that one day, when Beethoven was spending time with his fellow composer Ferdinand Ries, they saw a shepherd playing a pipe. They both could see it, but only Ries could hear its beauty. Then Beethoven had, for the first time, confronted his deafness. That incident had changed him forever.

Beethoven was slowly but surely going deaf but would not give up. He knew that the only thing he could do in life was related to music, and there was no way he would let that go. As a result, he continued to write music.

In the early stages of his deafness, he began to use lower notes, as he could not hear the higher ones so well, but once he went completely deaf, he could rely only on the sounds inside his mind.

Beethoven wrote many great pieces during his lifetime, but one of his most famous is his Ninth Symphony. That symphony was written when he was completely deaf. Life without music was not an option for him.

https://gedground.com/short-motivational-stories-of-failure-and-success-that-you-must-know/ Victor Step

**Things to Ponder**

The story of Ludwig van Beethoven and the men above exemplifies that regardless of our difficulty, we should never give up on our dreams. One of the secrets to success is that if we *"fail"* seven times, we try an eight, nine, and tenth.

*"It is impossible to live without failing at something unless you live so cautiously that you might as well not have lived*

*at all, in which case you have failed by default." – J.K. Rowling.*

Am I driven to improve, grow, and succeed, or do I quit when things become demanding or challenging?

"The one who falls and
gets up is stronger than the one
who never tried.
Do not fear failure but rather
fear not trying."
- Roy T. Bennett

## *Steve Jobs*

### *(February 24, 1955 – October 5, 2011)*

We all know Steve Jobs as the creator of the iPhone, iPod, iPad, and the Mac.

Jobs was born in San Francisco and was adopted at birth. Throughout his early life, he traveled to India and learned how to meditate. He says that "finding himself" was crucial to his future success, as that showed him that upon returning to the States, he must concentrate on doing what he loves.

Jobs co-founded Apple in 1976 in his parents' garage when he was only 21 years old. At the age of 23, he was already a millionaire. All of this happened after he dropped out of Reed College. In 1983 the Apple company was already a part of the Fortune 500. That same year, he recruited John Sculley, head of Pepsi-Cola, as Apple's new chief executive. There is even a famous quote that Jobs said to Sculley when hiring: *"Do you want to spend the rest of your life selling sugared water, or do you want a chance to change the world?"*.

Jobs was known to be very harsh and difficult to work with, but that was the quality he needed to create something as big as Apple. Nevertheless, soon enough, things got a little more complicated. Jobs and Sculley had their own differences regarding how things should be handled at Apple; complaints came towards Jobs from his workers, and as a result, the Macintosh group was taken away from Jobs' responsibilities. That left Jobs feeling powerless, and soon enough, he resigned from Apple.

In 1985, Jobs suffered from a mid-life crisis, which actually motivated him to co-launch a new computer company called "NeXT." NeXT did pretty much what Apple was supposed to do – it created a powerful computer. From this, it was clear that it wasn't about the companies but rather about the person creating them – Steve Jobs.

In 1996, Apple was not doing so well but decided to acquire NeXT. Ironically, Jobs was returned to the company that he had built and a year later became its CEO. The iPhone and iPad were about to come. I am sure you know the story of what happened then.

I hope these short motivational stories show you that no success is possible without failure. It is almost like a golden rule that in order to reach the top of the mountain, you need to struggle first. That is just how life is. As said in the beginning, what separates successful people from the ordinary is their will to try again and again despite adversity and failure.

https://gedground.com/short-motivational-stories-of-failure-and-success-that-you-must-know/ Victor Step

## Things to Ponder

It is not whether we will ever experience *"failure"* in our lives but when, where, and how often. More importantly, our perspective and reaction to it will go a long way in determining the outcome of our failures.

As previously mentioned, view failure as a negative ordeal or burden; give in, and you will fail. However, it becomes an impetus for success when seen and used as an opportunity to learn and grow.

What is my response to failure?

# Stress, Worry & Anxiety

*"In three words, I can sum up everything I've learned about life: It goes on."*
-Robert Frost

"Stress, worry, and anxiety" are the three emotions humanity has lived with from the cave days to the present. It seems we cannot get rid of these. But we can make our lives much easier if we understand that these are thoughts and perceptions we conjure up in our brains.

In most cases, they are the by-product of our thinking, engaging our minds in some past or future thing or event that we have little or no control over as it's either history or may or may not happen.

Some state that stress builds endurance. But the reality is that persistent and continuous stress, worry, or anxiety is detrimental to our well-being, as it releases chemicals into our bodies that will adversely affect our health.

As per the internet and AI, stress, worry, and anxiety are defined as tormenting oneself or suffering from disturbing thoughts arising from a general response to challenges, demands, or threats. It is the cognitive process of thinking about potential problems, uncertainties, and adverse outcomes. It is a heightened emotional and physiological state characterized by excessive fear, apprehension, and unease.[1]

A solution to curtailing and easing our disturbing thoughts is to prepare our mental state against the negative connotations of our thoughts. This is partly achieved by becoming informed and understanding the roots of the thoughts that cause us stress, worry, and anxiety. We then proactively use our schooled minds to abate our negative sentiments and emotions.

Lastly, once we earnestly address a concern, a further empowering step to living a calmer, quieter, less upsetting life is to let go of wanted outcomes and trust that things will turn out how they should.

*"Worry never robs*
*tomorrow of its sorrow,*
*it only saps today of its joy."*
—Leo F. Buscaglia

## *The Weight of Glass*

Once upon a time, a psychology professor walked around on a stage while teaching stress management principles to an auditorium filled with students.

As she raised a glass of water, everyone expected they'd be asked the typical "*glass half empty or glass half full*" question. Instead, with a smile on her face, the professor asked, "*How heavy is this glass of water I'm holding?*"

Students shouted out answers ranging from eight ounces to a couple of pounds. She replied, "*From my perspective, the absolute weight of this glass doesn't matter. It all depends on how long I hold it.*

*If I hold it for a minute or two, it's fairly light.*
*If I hold it for an hour straight, its weight might make my arm ache a little.*
*If I hold it for a day straight, my arm will likely cramp up and feel completely numb and paralyzed, forcing me to drop the glass to the floor.*

*In each case, the weight of the glass doesn't change, but the longer I hold it, the heavier it feels to me.*"

As the class shook their heads in agreement, she continued, *"Your <u>stresses and worries</u> in life are very much like this glass of water.*

*Think about them for a while, and nothing happens. Think about them a bit longer, and you begin to ache a little. Think about them all day long, and you will feel completely numb and paralyzed — incapable of doing anything else until you drop them."*

<u>https://philipchircop.wordpress.com/</u> *Short Stories Of Inspiration & Motivation Chris Blenning (2018)*

## Things to Ponder!

*"The Weight of Glass"* points out that the more you think about or hold on to something, the more *"stressful"* it becomes.

As per Robert Frost's quote, life *"It goes on,"* no matter what, it is essential to learn to conquer or mitigate our burdensome concerns if we are to live a healthy, happy life. It is not that successful individuals and winners are not vulnerable to negative stimuli.

It is that they *learn* to mitigate, assuage, or conquer *troublesome_thoughts* with knowledge, introspection, reflection, and *letting go* since they understand that nothing good is derived from spending time on debilitating emotions and energies.

Am I a stressed, worried, or anxious person?

    If yes, why?

    How can I overcome this?

"*Stress, worry, anxiety often give a small thing a big shadow.*"
- HCJ

# *The Burden*

Two monks were returning to the monastery in the evening. It had rained, and there were puddles of water on the road sides.

A beautiful young woman was standing in one place, unable to walk across because of a puddle of water. The elder of the two monks went up to her, lifted her, left her on the other side of the road, and continued his way to the monastery.

In the evening the younger monk came to the elder monk and said, "Sir, as monks, we cannot touch a woman?" The elder monk answered, "Yes, brother."

Then the younger monk asks again, "But then, Sir, how is that you lifted that woman on the roadside?" The elder monk smiled at him and said, "I left her on the other side of the road, but you are still carrying her."

https://innerspacetherapy.in/the-burden-story-stop-worrying/

## Things to Ponder!

"The Burden" is a perfect example of how we go through life preoccupied, *"worried, and anxious"* with the verbal comments or actions of others or what others think of us or our actions.

More often than not, this is of zero value to us. Since one is robbed of precious time wasted in meaningless thoughts and zapped of vital energy and better health spent elsewhere.

Am I concerned with how others view or judge me? If "yes," why?

Do I hold on to worrisome or anxiety-provoking thoughts?

If "yes," how can I overcome this detrimental mindset?

# Integrity & Trust

> "*Integrity gives you real freedom because,*
> *you have nothing to fear since you*
> *have nothing to hide.*"
> – *Zig Ziglar*

Perhaps the most essential insight or resource that shapes the plane of our existence is living our lives from *integral wisdom*. At the core of who we are, there is this moral compass that, if we tune in, will efficaciously guide us through life's perils and success.

We tap into this inherent pathfinder by being present and aware of our environment, reflecting on our life's journey, circumstances, and issues, and discerning what matters that is important, invaluable, and solemnly life-affirming from all that isn't.

We then honor our authenticity by being truthful and righteous with all; this is the path of least resistance, peace of mind, and great fortunes.

In a nutshell, *"integrity" is the adherence to moral and ethical principles, honesty, and trustworthiness despite temptations or challenges.* It is the state of being whole, complete, and undiminished. It promotes consistency, accountability, and fairness.

Without integrity, success does not exist, only a superficial, empty illusion. Integral individuals inspire respect and confidence from others and foster positive relationships.[1]

"*Integrity is
doing what is right
and truthful, regardless of
the consequences.*"

*– Unknown*

## *Easy Eddie*

Al Capone owned virtually all of Chicago in the 1920s. He had a net worth of more than one billion, funded by his organized crime, including murder, prostitution, and bootlegging. Capone's lawyer, nicknamed *"Easy Eddie,"* promoted Capone's continued dominance. Easy Eddie's skills kept Al Capone out of the prison sentences that Capone deserved.

Capone showered Easy Eddie in excess for keeping him out of jail. Easy Eddie had every luxury available. Easy Eddie's estate filled an entire city block. Eddie ignored being awash in evil because of the lifestyle it afforded. His heart was hard, except for Eddie's one soft spot — a son he loved completely. He wanted his son to have every advantage Eddie didn't have while growing up.

Despite everything he had was the fruit of crime, Eddie attempted to teach his son morals. Eddie wanted his son to be a more honorable man than Eddie. But with all of his influence and wealth, there were two things Eddie couldn't pass on to his son — his example and good name.

Eddie was faced with the question, *"What good is it for a man to gain the whole world and lose his soul?"*

That question provoked Eddie. He began to change. Easy Eddie chose to make his wrongs right.

Eddie tried to clean up his name by telling the police the truth about Al Capone. That required Easy Eddie to witness against Capone and his organized crime syndicate.

Eddie testified, and within a year, the mob murdered Easy Eddie. He died after a tremendous flash of gunfire on a desolate Chicago street. But his life was not in vain. He had given riches to his son worth more than an estate. Eddie gave him integrity.

https://community.thriveglobal.com/two-stories-of-integrity/
Hamilton Lindley Pub. Feb. 22. 2021

## Things to Ponder!

Through his actions, "Easy Eddie" demonstrates that it is never too late to own your mistakes, make amends, and do what is right. *"Integrity"* is being whole, complete, ethical, and, most notably, at peace with all.

Do I stand up for what is right?
  If "yes," how?    If "no," why not?

Do I succumb to difficult or alluring circumstances?

    If "yes," why?

"*Integrity is the cornerstone of success.*"

*– John D. MacDonald*

## *Butch O'Hare*

World War II revealed many heroes. One was a fighter pilot named Butch O'Hare. His hero story started after being airborne with the rest of his squadron. Butch looked at his fuel gauge and, to his surprise, saw that the groundcrew had not refilled Butch's fuel tank. So Butch would not have enough fuel to complete the mission and return to the aircraft carrier.

Butch's commander ordered Butch to return to the ship immediately. He did so grudgingly. As Butch returned, he saw a sight that turned his blood cold. An enemy squadron was racing to the American ships. With the entire division on a mission, the whole American fleet was defenseless. Butch had no chance to bring back his squadron, and he couldn't warn the fleet of impending peril.

So Butch decided there was only one thing he could do — divert the enemy from the fleet.

Ignoring his safety, he plunged into the Japanese formation, firing his guns as he stunned enemy planes.

The Japanese airplanes fired on him from all angles with their fierce machine guns and cannons. Butch just kept moving.

After his winged guns emptied all their ammunition, Butch dove his aircraft towards the enemy aircraft, attempting to clip an enemy wing and send them down in a spiral. Ultimately, the shocked Japanese squadron changed directions.

Butch O'Hare returned to the carrier. Once he landed, Butch told of his adventure. And the movie from Butch's gun-camera showed the tale. Butch shot down five Japanese aircraft. Butch was the Navy's first flying ace of World War II. He was the first Naval Aviator to win the Congressional Medal of Honor. Butch was killed a year later, at age 29.

Butch's hometown was proud of his name, and today O'Hare Airport in Chicago is named for this American hero.

https://community.thriveglobal.com/two-stories-of-integrity/

Hamilton Lindley Pub. Feb. 22. 2021

## Things to Ponder!

These stories have an underlying common denominator. And that is that Butch O'Hare was "Easy Eddie's" son. Easy

Eddie not only gave Butch the lesson of integrity. But also a good name.

Eddie understood that he had to infuse his son Butch with the truth instead of living a dishonorable life. *Honesty is what one may say, but integrity is how one shows it; it's action-oriented, not word-oriented.*[2]

Easy Eddie showed reform and valued integrity despite his probable outcome of death. That integrity inspired his son Butch to do the same thing.

Winners know that success without integrity has no lasting, rewarding value, leaving one with an empty, hollow taste.

Do I live an integral life?
　　If "yes," how?
　　If "no," what deters me from doing so?

---

[2] https://community.thriveglobal.com/two-stories-of-integrity/ Hamilton Lindley Pub. Feb. 22. 2021

# Trust

> *"Trust is the glue of life. It's the most essential ingredient in effective communication. It's the foundational principle that holds all relationships."*
> - Stephen Covey

"*Trust*" is a fundamental concept that is vital in our relationships and interactions. It provides us with predictability, security, and cooperation in all aspects of life.

Trust relies on the belief, confidence, *integrity*, and reliability that a person, group, institution, company, or government will meet our expectations. It comprises credence, certainty, and reliance, usually learned, earned, or derived from personal or historical experience.

For example, an *individual's trust* relies on honesty, loyalty, dependability, and promises. *Self-trust* is an individual's confidence and belief in their own decisions, abilities, and judgments. It is essential for well-being and personal growth.

*Social trust* exists between a society or community as a whole, and *institutional trust* is people's trust in companies, governments, and institutions and their ability to act in the public's best interest.

Lastly, trust is often seen as the foundation upon which emotional intimacy, effective communication, and cooperation are built-in relationships. Without trust, relationships may suffer from suspicion, fear, and a lack of openness.[1]

*"Trust is earned when actions meet words."*

*- Destiny Duprey*

## *The Baker and Farmer*

A long time ago, a baker and a farmer lived in the same small English village. These two men had a friendly arrangement in place. The farmer would sell a pound of butter to the baker each day. And, each day, the baker would give the farmer a pound loaf of bread in exchange.

One morning, the baker decided to weigh the butter to see if he'd actually received the correct amount of a full pound of butter.

To his surprise, he discovered that the farmer had sold him less butter than he'd paid for. Angry about the unfairness, he took the farmer to court.

At the hearing, the judge asked the farmer whether he used any measure to weigh the butter.

*"Your Honor, I am but a lowly farmer and do not own a proper measure. I simply use an old-fashioned scale,"* he replied.

How do you weigh the butter then, inquired the judge.

To this, the farmer answered:

*"Your Honor, long before the baker started buying butter from my farm, I've been buying a pound loaf of*

*bread from him. Every day, when he brings me the bread, I place it on my scale and give him the same weight in butter. If anyone is to be blamed, it's the baker."*

https://www.godsotherways.com/stories/2020/3/25/do-the-next-thing-4baw5-8faz4-8858t-9sdzk-syg98 Gods Other Ways, Donna Kersey – Author Unknown

## Things to Ponder!

Looking back at our early childhood, we can surmise that being *"trustworthy"* is our inherent nature. Then, as people, life, and rationality conjure upon us, doubt, greed, imperfection, and malice permeate our flawlessness.

"The Baker and the Farmer" story highlights the importance of trustful relations built on honesty, fairness, integrity, and loyalty. Unfortunately, verification is sometimes a must due to our learned fallacious behaviors.

How do I build trust with others?
In my personal and business relationships, do I have to verify trust?
If yes, how does this make me feel?

"To be trusted is
a greater compliment than
being loved."

- George MacDonald

# The Bond

A little girl and her father were crossing a bridge. The father was kind of scared, so he asked his little daughter, *"Sweetheart, please hold my hand so that you don't fall into the river."*

The little girl said, *"No, Dad. You hold my hand."*
*"What's the difference?"* Asked the puzzled father.
*"There's a big difference,"* replied the little girl.

*"If I hold your hand and something happens to me, chances are that I may let your hand go."*
*"But if you hold my hand, I know for sure that no matter what happens, you will never let my hand go."*

**Things to Ponder!**

There are situations when *"trust"* is a given. But more often than not, establishing trust requires one to dedicate time to building and cultivating truthful, in-depth relationships.

In "Fully Human," Susan Packard's book on emotional fitness, she shares five fast tips for building trust. They are: *become self-aware*—know your capabilities; *be honest*—

with others, so they do not question your authenticity; *be steady*—do not have a yo-yo temper, character, or disposition; *be dependable*—others must know that they can count on you, and finally, *be proactive*—take the initiative as a problem solver, helper, trust builder.

Lastly, "The Bond" shares with us that in relationships, *the essence of trust is not in its binding but in its bond.* So hold the hand of the person who loves you rather than expecting them to grab yours.

Do others see me as a trustworthy individual?

If "yes," how?

If "no," why not?

How do I demonstrate that I trust others?

# Empowerment

> *"Empowerment is not a gift.*
> *It's a shift in perspective."*
> *- Bryant McGill*

There is no success, winning, or happiness without "*empowerment*." It is about intellectually, emotionally, spiritually, and physically working on your being, recognizing your worth, manifesting your destiny, and inspiring and helping others to do the same.

It requires a shift in perception from living a life based on scarce resources, where there is not enough to go around; therefore, I must take mine while I can, to understanding that we partake in a bountiful environment, earth, with plenty for all. We draw from life as we learn, think, comprehend, and share.

Specifically, *empowerment* enables one with the ability, knowledge, permission, authority, confidence, or resources to take control of one's life and achieve one's goals. It often involves providing support, education, and opportunities and removing obstacles hindering someone else's progress.

## The Essence of Winners – *Empowerment*

Empowerment manifests in all life contexts, including personal development, workplace environments, communities, and social or political movements. It's a concept that aims to promote equality, autonomy, and a sense of agency, ultimately leading to increased self-esteem, resilience, and positive outcomes.[1]

"*Everything
you want is just outside of
your comfort zone.*"

*- Robert Allen*

# *The Man in the Arena*

It is not the critic who counts, not the man who points
out how the strong man stumbles or where the doer
of deeds could have done them better.

The credit belongs to the man who is actually
in the arena.
Whose face is marred by dust and sweat and blood.
Who strives valiantly, who errs, who comes short
again and again, because there is no effort
without error and shortcomings.

But he who does actually strive to do the deeds.
Who knows great enthusiasms, the great devotions;
who spends himself in a worthy cause.

Who, at best, knows in the end the triumph of high
achievement,
and who, at worst, if he fails, at least fails while
daring greatly.
So that his place shall never be with those cold and
timid souls
who neither know victory nor defeat.

Theodore Roosevelt, Excerpt from the speech "Citizen In A Republic,"
Delivered at the Sorbonne, in Paris, France on 23 April, 1910

**Things to Ponder!**

*"Empowerment"* is an energy, notion, or concept that inspires us to better our lives and the lives of others. For some, it is a natural disposition or perception of life. Some learn it through grit, personal experiences, observation, or emulation of successful people.

There are those who choose not to partake, for they are content living a poor or mediocre lifestyle and erroneously believe that empowering themselves or others is too difficult or complex, not their responsibility, or will rob them of something. Figure that!

Do I believe in empowerment?

What empowers me?

Do I empower others?

    If "yes," how?

## - Triumphant Fundamentals -

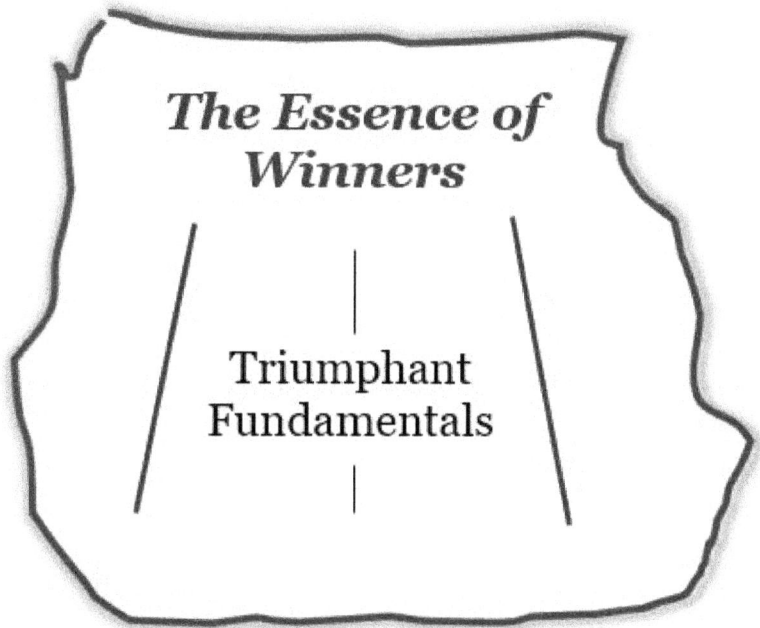

### The Essence of Winners

Triumphant
Fundamentals

*"The seeds of triumph lie within*
*our fundamentals."*

- HCJ

# Goals

> *"Setting goals is the first step in turning the invisible into the visible."*
> - Tony Robbins

Whether personal, social, professional, business, government, or country-related, all *"goals"* have a commonality. That is *"achievement"* towards which effort is directed.[1]

Since birth, most of us have an internal need to accomplish, move forward, and improve our being and status.

As infants, the innate goal is to gain our loved one's care and love; thereby, we smile.

We attend pre-k and elementary school, and the goal is still to please our parents and teachers through good behavior, attaining good grades, and making friends.

In high school, our goals become more defined as we add the future possibility of long-term relationships, having children, higher education, becoming a doctor, nurse, lawyer, business professional, artist, attending a trade school, or becoming a professional athlete. As we know, the options are endless.

Most of our goals are defined early in life. Many achieve their goals, while many others either fail or live a life of discontent. The question then becomes, what do achievers know or do differently from those who consistently struggle or fail?

The simple answer is that some might need to clarify the goals, adjust the approach, or even define alternative goals. Others might need to brush up or learn new skills and concepts. Achieving *success* in today's ever-changing, competitive world encompasses patience, discipline, perseverance, and embracing challenges and opportunities.

"A goal,
without a plan, is just
a wish."
- Anonymous

# The Tiny Frog

Once upon a time, there was a group of tiny frogs who arranged a competition. The _goal_ was to reach the top of a tower. A massive crowd of frogs gathered to watch the race. The race began.

Not one frog in the audience believed the contestants would reach the top. After all, it was a HUGE tower!

The crowd grew, and many yelled, *"This is too difficult!" "They will NEVER make it to the top." "Not a chance that they will succeed. The tower is too high!"*

One by one, the tiny frogs collapsed and fell off the tower. Still, a group of determined frogs climbed higher and higher. But the crowd continued to yell, *"This is too difficult! No one will make it!"* Discouraged and convinced by the negative cries, more tiny frogs collapsed and fell off the tower.

Some of the frogs still climbing complained of the pain and eventually gave up. While others, tired and battered, heard their peers' complaints and subsequently threw in the towel.

In the midst of this, one tiny frog persisted. He climbed and climbed. This tiny frog seemed to have super-frog strength that allowed him to push forward in spite of others failing. *"Why, though? Why is he able to climb so far when others are failing?"* the crowd wondered.

By now, all the tiny frogs had either collapsed or given up — except for that one tiny frog. The crowd continued to yell, now only at that tiny frog, *"This is too difficult!" "You will NEVER make it to the top!" "Not a chance that you will succeed. The tower is too high!"*

But for some reason, that tiny frog climbed further, seemingly unaffected. Finally, he reached his destination, the top.

All the tiny frogs were amazed at how this one frog could reach the top. They crowded around him, wanting to know his secret. *As it turned out, he was deaf.*

https://personalexcellence.co/blog/frog/ By Celestine Chua

**Things to Ponder!**

Reaching one's *"goals"* might be difficult and require considerable time and effort, but as winners know, depending on the goal, it is emotionally, physically, and financially rewarding and empowering.

"The Tiny Frog" demonstrates what is obtainable by being committed and knowledgeable about the subject matter, breaking down the goal into small manageable steps, making adjustments as needed, and diligently working until its culmination.

The story also points out that there could be many naysayers, discouragements, and critics along the way. *"You cannot do this!" "It is impossible!" "You will never succeed." "You're too young for this." "You're too old for this." "You are not good enough." "You should quit."*

Some will be upset, give up, or try to convince the critics that they are wrong. Still others persist, albeit sometimes with less enthusiasm.

Unless constructive opinions, when dealing with detractors, complainers, and negative stimuli, ignore them. *"Turn a deaf ear."*

Time spent addressing or even thinking about pessimistic comments is precious seconds taken away from progress on your goal.

As the owner of your goal, the only important thing is to focus on your vision and pursue it relentlessly.

Once you have achieved your objective, you have conquered and validated yourself. *WON!*

What are my goals?

Do I accomplish them or fall short?

    If I fail, why and how can I  change this?

# Risk & Courage

*"The biggest risk is not taking risks.*
*In a world that's changing quickly,*
*the only strategy that is guaranteed to*
*fail is not taking risks."*
*– Mark Zuckerberg*

Throughout our lives, most of us have been taught or learned to avoid taking risks. That is exposing ourselves to lost, hazard, danger, or injury.

Specifically, *"risk"* refers to the possible failure inherent in an uncertain path, choice, decision, or endeavor. It involves the probability of harm or negative result from an action, decision, situation, or event one participates in.[1]

Even though one should be prudent, careful, and responsible in guarding against health-related risks or bodily injury, the same cannot be said when living most of our lives.

*Risk* is an ingrained and vital part of life and progress, often leading us to personal and material growth, new opportunities, and success. Everyone has heard the phrase, *"No risk, No reward."* Partaking in education, entrepreneurship, vocational, financial, professional, or business ventures will ultimately pay off.

One might ask what differentiates the seemingly successful risk-taker from everyone else, and how can one mitigate risk and turn the odds of success in our favor?

The answer to both of these questions is simple. First, *the effective risk-taker never takes risks lightly*. They know that life is perilous and nothing worthwhile is easy, free, or guaranteed.

Secondly, they are willing to pay the piper to grow and reach greater heights by intellectually and emotionally evaluating the possibility of different outcomes and the potential impact of those outcomes, engaging in *calculated or managed risk*, thereby diminishing the liabilities and giving themselves an opportunity at success.

*"If you are not willing to risk the unusual, you will have to settle for the ordinary."*

— *Jim Rohn*

## *The Value of Taking Risks And Perseverance: Lessons Learnt From "The Third Door"*

Picture this: you're standing outside the grand nightclub of life, where each door presents a different pathway to success.

First, there's the First Door. It's the one everyone knows about, the entrance where the masses queue up, hoping for their chance to step inside. The air is filled with anticipation but also with uncertainty. You watch as some are granted entry while others are turned away, realizing that success here is a game of chance.

Then, there's the Second Door. It's the VIP entrance, reserved for the selected few who possess the right connections, pedigree, or perhaps just the right stroke of luck.

But amidst the hustle and bustle, there's the Third Door. It's the one that often goes unnoticed, dismissed, or simply overlooked. It's unconventional, hidden in plain sight, and requires a unique blend of creativity, persistence, and audacity to discover and utilize. This Third Door represents the unorthodox paths that lead to extraordinary success — the paths less traveled.

# Introduction

Ever wondered what sets apart the world's most successful individuals from the rest of us? Well, hold onto your hats because I stumbled upon an absolute gem called "The Third Door" by Alex Banayan.

Now, I usually shy away from writing book reviews — I find them a bit too mainstream — but this one is a game-changer, and it's all about *embracing risks!*

In his revelatory book, Alex Banayan beautifully captures the essence of this metaphor:

*"Many times, the hardest part about achieving a dream isn't actually achieving it — it's stepping through your fear of the unknown when you don't have a plan."*

# How It All Began

Banayan's journey commenced with the curiosity of a college student who was uncertain about his future. Determined to unlock the secrets of success, he embarked on a quest to interview luminaries across various fields. From business moguls to entertainment icons, he sought to understand their paths to greatness. Instead of waiting passively for opportunities to arise, Banayan took bold and unconventional approaches —

knocking on doors, crashing events, and pushing boundaries to secure interviews.

## Lessons learned

### *The Power of Taking Risks*

Banayan's journey underscores the importance of taking risks. Instead of waiting for opportunities, he actively sought them out, demonstrating that success often requires boldness and initiative. For instance, when he sought to interview Bill Gates, he didn't just send an email and hope for the best. Instead, he camped outside a conference venue for days, persistently pursuing an opportunity to speak with Gates. This audacious approach paid off, leading to a conversation that would shape his path to success.

### *Embrace Rejection*

Banayan's story and the stories of the people he interviewed show readers that rejection isn't the end — it's just part of the journey. Every no gets you closer to a yes, and resilience is crucial. An illustrative example is his encounter with Larry King. Initially rebuffed by King's team, Banayan persisted, sending letters and emails until he finally secured a meeting.

### *Think Outside the Box*

The idea of the Third Door itself is a call to think creatively and look for opportunities in unconventional places. Sometimes, the best paths aren't the most obvious ones, and innovation can lead to unexpected successes. Banayan describes it perfectly: *"When you change what you believe is possible, you change what becomes possible."*

## Persistence and Audacity

Banayan's relentless persistence and audacity were instrumental in securing interviews with influential figures. His willingness to push boundaries and defy norms serves as a reminder of the importance of *perseverance* in achieving one's goals. For instance, he embodied the "kissing the frog" theory advocated by inventor Dean Kamen, tirelessly pursuing opportunities despite rejections, adapting his approach along the way.

*Dean Kamen came up with a metaphor for persistence: kissing frogs. Based on the princess and the frog fairy tale. It describes a mentality by which you kiss frogs (potential solutions to your problem) until one of them reveals itself as a prince — the right solution.*

## The Value of Creativity

Banayan's unconventional approaches, such as camping outside conference venues and crashing events, highlight the value of creativity in problem-solving. Thinking outside the box can uncover hidden opportunities and pave the way for success.

## *Learning from Failure*

Throughout his journey, Banayan faced rejection and criticism. Yet, instead of letting failure deter him, he used it as a catalyst for growth. This ability to bounce back from setbacks is essential for overcoming obstacles on the path to success.

## Conclusion

In a world where success often seems reserved for the lucky few, "The Third Door" offers a refreshing perspective. *Banayan's journey is a testament to the power of taking risks, embracing uncertainty, and daring to pursue your dreams with passion and determination.*

Through his bold and unconventional approach, Banayan demonstrates that success is not simply about waiting for opportunities to come to you — *it's about actively seeking them out and being willing to take risks along the way.* By embracing uncertainty, pushing boundaries, and persisting in the face of challenges, we can unlock the doors to extraordinary opportunities and achieve our goals against all odds.

So, the next time you find yourself standing at the grand nightclub of life, faced with a choice of doors, remember the wisdom of "The Third Door." Dare to step outside your comfort zone, embrace the unknown, and pursue your dreams with courage and conviction. Who knows what extraordinary adventures and opportunities await on the other side?

https://eeshakamat.medium.com/the-value-of-taking-risks-and-perseverance-lessons-learnt-from-the-third-door-0314b8650cb2

Eesha Kamat 5/20/24

## Things to Ponder!

At times, excelling, succeeding, and winning require *"risking"* the known or comfortable and reaching for one's dreams. Remember that the possibility of undesirable outcomes is innate within jeopardous decisions, situations, and actions; hence, *always do your homework and then reach for the stars.*

Am I a risk taker?   If *"Yes,"* how?   If *"no,"* why not?

# Courage

> *"Fear is a reaction. Courage is a decision."*
> *- Winston Churchill*

We will experience situations that challenge us to make difficult and even life-altering choices. Some faint-hearted people will run away, ignore the risk at their own or someone else's peril, while others reluctantly engage it.

Then there are those who willingly, without much thought, respond to the threat. Usually, these individuals do not see their actions as courageous but as just their duty. For them, there never was, or is, a choice. Their disposition to fearlessly respond to the assailing stimulus is inherent.

For most of us, *"Courage"* is a fundamental human trait, the quality of mind or spirit that involves the strength to confront fear, danger, pain, uncertainty, or adversity. It is the ability to act in the face of difficulties, challenges, or potential harm, even when one feels afraid or anxious.

In its simplest form, courage is going to bed mentally or physically depleted, exhausted, or infirm, having given your all, yet rising the next day to proceed anew. Courage is not knowing what life has in store for us but choosing to continue to fight, partake, and invest in it.

*Courage is not the absence of fear but the ability to persevere and act despite it.*

Personal growth is usually attained when we courageously participate in the demanding, arduous, risky, or painful. We must face our fears to live an empowering, successful life, as the alternative can be restrictive and unsatisfying.

As per Dictionary.com and ChatGPT, there are various forms of courage, including;

*Physically* confronting bodily pain, discomfort, and danger, such as risking one's life to protect others from harm.

*Moral* courage is about doing what is right, just, or ethical, even when it goes against societal norms, personal interests, or the pressure to conform. It involves standing up for one's principles and values, even if it means facing criticism or backlash.

*Emotional* courage involves being vulnerable and open to feelings, expressing oneself honestly, and expressing sentiments in personal relationships.

*Intellectual* courage is the willingness to challenge prevailing beliefs, question established ideas, and explore new possibilities, even if it means facing skepticism or rejection from others.

In summary, courage enables individuals to overcome obstacles, pursue personal growth, and contribute positively to society. It is admired and respected because it requires strong determination and willingness to stand for what is right, just, or meaningful.[1]

"*Courage is
the virtue that allows
us to conquer and make our
dreams possible.*"
- HCJ

## *Switching Careers*

What do you want to be when you grow up? This is a daunting question we get asked often when we're kids. Then, we get asked things related to marriage, kids, and money. But what if the thing you thought you wanted to be when you grew up is not the thing that your adult self is meant to do? Oh, oh, hello, fear.

I grew up as the artist of the family; we all knew I was going to pursue a creative career that would involve color in some way. Painting, designing, and coming up with creative ideas were my things. My life was set. I evolved from painter to designer to art director to brand strategist, four different careers in the same realm as people would've predicted since I was a kid.

What people, or even I, couldn't predict was the path that awaited me.

The next thing I know, I'm standing on a TEDx stage, sharing a project I had embarked on. And without even noticing it, I became a "Motivational Speaker" that day. Companies, schools, and organizations started inviting me to speak at their events.

My website michellepoler.com, went from showcasing ads and brands to demo-reels and testimonials. My business card went from eight colors to three, and I started comparing myself to other speakers. Honestly, I felt like an impostor, hoping not to get caught during my next presentation.

I. freaked out.

*I'm no Brene Brown,* I thought. *I'm no Simon Sinek or Tony Robbins. Why would anyone want to listen to what I had to say?*

My impostor syndrome was taking over me. So, I did what I know how to do best: brand myself.

I realized that I couldn't begin to compare myself to other professional speakers. That's when I remembered one of the key learnings from my branding days, *"USP."* Unique selling Proposition. *What makes me unique?* I asked myself.

1. My background in design gives me the skills and the eye to craft nice slides – I watched dozens of TED Talks, and even the best ones had terrible slides.

2. My Venezuelan accent and choppy English can be either embarrassing, interestingly cool, different, or unique. I choose the latter

3. Finally, I can't stand high heels, fake eyelashes, or any kind of business attire.

So I branded myself as a young, up-and-coming speaker with colorful, hand-drawn slides, cool sneakers, cropped tops, a relatable vibe, and a memorable opening that *may or may not* include hardcore reggeaton dancing.

Dancing "Vaivén" by Daddy Yankee at the International Student Leadership Conference in Rome.

I embraced the things that made me different to become my authentic self on stage and wow an audience my way. I learned that the only way to defeat the impostor syndrome and gain the confidence to believe in ourselves is by differentiating instead of comparing.

Comparison leads to lower self-esteem, depression and makes us doubt our skills and potential.

So, take a moment to think about your USP. Embrace those little things that make you different, and own the real you.

PS: Remember, have fun. Don't take yourself too seriously :)

*"Our job in this lifetime is not to shape ourselves into some ideal we imagine we ought to be. But to find out who we already are, and become it." – Steven Pressfield, The War of Art.*

https://www.hellofears.com/stories/courage-is-switching-careers Michele Poler, 29, Nomad

**Things to Ponder!**

We use multiple excuses to keep us within our comfort zone. But other than for mental or physical relaxation, these pretexts stifle or prevent our opportunities for growth and prosperity.

The *"courageous"* may encounter many disappointments, experience profound disillusionment, and gather many wounds but are proud of their scars; they represent emblems of a truly phenomenal life.

*"The fearful, cautious, cynical, and self-repressed do not live at all. And that is simply no way to be in this world."* —Anthon St. Maarten.

What excuses, if any, do I use to stop me from taking a leap of faith towards fulfilling my dreams?

*"Courage is never to let your actions be influenced by your fears."*

*- Arthur Koestler*

## *RIGHT over EASY*

Yes, when saving even one life matters. Imagine having saved hundreds of lives just because you had the courage to do the right thing instead of the easy thing. This is the story of a ship in the middle of a shipwreck and a lifeboat that reached in time.

There were three ships around this sinking ship when the distress signal was being sent. The first one, Sampson, was approx. Seven miles away from the sinking ship. Only 7 miles!

They could see the sinking ship! But they turned their backs. Why? Because the crew aboard the ship had been involved in illegal hunting of seals. They turned their backs to a shipwreck because they didn't want to get caught.

Sometimes, courage is not about insane bravery. It's just simply about having the guts to let go of what's important to you because someone else is in dire need. Obviously, the crew of Sampson did not possess this royal quality.

There was another ship approximately 14 miles away from our sinking ship. The Californian saw the distress signals as they were within eyeshot, but they were surrounded by ice, and it was nighttime, so it wasn't probably comfortable for them to move.

They decided to wait till the morning for the conditions to improve. You know that '20 seconds of insane courage' we often talk about? When it is about someone else, those 20s become even more important!

The third ship was approximately 58 miles away and was already moving in the other direction, but when they heard the cries over the radio, they decided to be the lifeboat. The captain of this ship just prayed to God for direction and turned his boat. They waded through ice fields in the dark but kept going.

This lifeboat was Carpathia. And the shipwreck it sailed to was none other than the Titanic.

They saved a whopping 705 lives that night. Those 705 lives were saved because one man chose the right over the easy. That one man had the courage to look beyond his comfort. And the man deserves to be acknowledged. He is Captain Arthur Rostron, the man who simply said, *"Mr. Dean. Turn the ship around."*

https://akashgautam.com/2018/10/17/three-super-inspirational-real-life-stories-of-courage/ - Akash Gautam

**Things to Ponder!**

At its core, *"courage"* is comprised of integral and moral fortitude.

Whether physical, emotional, intellectual, or ethical, despite the circumstance, apprehension, or threat, throughout our lives, we will be confronted with the need for courage, to choose right over easy, and to stand for what is just.

The question for us is how do we respond. What must we do, or what do we need, to have the strength to respond affirmatively when courage beckons?

Have I ever had to demonstrate courage?
    If "yes," was I able to?
    How did I feel?
If I could not respond courageously, why not?
    How did I feel?

# Accountability, Responsibility & Commitment

> *"Blaming others gives your power away.*
> *Being accountable and responsible gives us*
> *the power to transform our life."*
> *— HCJ*

To assume *"accountability"* is to take *ownership* of one's actions, decisions, and obligations and fulfill our duties and commitments with transparency and integrity. It is a vital aspect of personal and social development.

It reinforces ethical behavior and trustworthiness within the overall functioning of the individual, society, organization, and government.

When we engage in self-defeating behavior by abdicating accountability, shirking our commitments, and being untruthful, we compromise our growth and prosperity with the negative repercussions that follow.

Some believe that being *answerable* for all our actions is more complex and arduous than not standing up for them. *The contrary is true.*

*Owning our choices and decisions and being truthful gives us a sense of worth, self-respect, and honor.* It simplifies our existence and rewards us with a more fulfilling, happier, prosperous journey—the difference between winning and losing.

"Accountability is
the glue that ties commitment
to result."

—Bob Proctor

## A Special Seed

A successful businessman was aging and knew the time had come to choose a successor to take over the business. Instead of choosing one of his directors or his children, he decided to do something different. He gathered all the young executives of his company.

He said: "*It is time for me to step down and choose the next chief executive.*" "*I have decided to choose one of you.*" The young executives were surprised, but the boss continued: "*Today, I will give each of you a very special seed.*"

"*I want you to plant the seed, water it, and return here in a year with what you have grown from the seed I gave you. Then I will judge the plants you bring, and the one I choose will be the next CEO.*"

A man named Jim was there that day, and he, like the others, received a seed. He returned home and excitedly told the story to his wife. She helped him get a pot, soil, and compost, and he planted the seed. Every day, I watered it and saw if it had grown. After about three weeks, some of the other executives started talking about their seeds and the plants that were beginning to grow.

Jim kept checking his seed, but nothing ever grew. Three weeks passed, four weeks, five weeks, and still nothing. By then, others were talking about their plants, but Jim had none and felt like a failure.

Six months passed, and still, there was nothing in Jim's boat. He simply knew that he had killed his seed. Everyone else had trees and tall plants, but he had nothing. Jim said nothing to his colleagues; However, he continued to water and fertilize the land. I so wanted the seed to grow.

A year passed, and the CEO asked the young executives to bring their plants to work to inspect them.

When Jim told his wife he wouldn't accept an empty boat, she asked him to be honest about what happened. Jim felt nauseous; it would be the most embarrassing moment of his life, but he knew his wife was right. He carried his empty boat to the meeting room.

When Jim arrived, he was surprised by the variety of plants the other executives were growing. They were beautiful, in all shapes and sizes. Jim put his empty pot on the ground, and many of his companions laughed. Some felt sorry for him!

When the CEO arrived, he surveyed the room and greeted his young executives. Jim just tried to hide in the back. *"Wow, what great plants, trees, and flowers you have grown,"* said the CEO. *"Today, one of you will be named the next CEO!"*

Suddenly, the CEO saw Jim at the back of the room with his empty pot. He asked Jim to come to the front of the room. Jim was terrified. He thought, *"The CEO knows I'm a failure! Maybe I'll get myself fired!*

When Jim got to the front, the CEO asked him what happened to his seed. Jim told him the story. The CEO asked everyone to sit down except Jim. He looked at Jim and then announced to the young executives, "*Here's your next CEO: Jim!*"

Jim couldn't believe it. Jim couldn't even grow his seed. "*How could I be the new CEO?*" said the others.

The CEO then said, "One year ago *today, I gave a seed to everyone in this room. I told you to take the seed, plant it, water it, and bring it to me today. But I gave you all cooked seeds; they were dead; "It was not possible for them to grow."*

"*All of you, except Jim, have brought me trees, plants, and flowers. When you discovered that the seed did not grow, you replaced the one I gave you with another. Jim was the only one who had the courage and honesty to bring me a pot of my seed. Therefore, he is the new CEO!*"

If you plant honesty, you will reap trust.
If you plant kindness, you will reap friends.
If you plant humility, you will reap greatness.

If you plant perseverance, you will reap contentment.
If you plant consideration, you will reap perspective.
If you sow hard work, you will reap success.
If you plant forgiveness, you will reap reconciliation.

*So be careful what you plant now; It will determine what you will harvest later.*

https://raycenter.wp.drake.edu/2013/02/22/a-very-special-seed-a-story-about-integrity/ The Robert D. and Billie Ray Center

## Things to ponder!

The story reflects the fact that you reap what you sow. It is best to be honest and *"accountable,"* as the negative consequences of lack of ownership, deceit, finger-pointing, and blaming are detrimental to our character and adversely affect an individual's and any organization's ability to operate effectively.

No matter how difficult or painful it could be, *there is no substitute for the truth.* Being accountable and avoiding deception gives us the peace and comfort of not having to remember compromising, embarrassing responses and situations.

*Aspiring to live a respected, rewarding, successful life requires us to choose the most fertile, advantageous path— the one paved by truth, accountability, and responsible living.*

Do I lack accountability?   Am I deceitful in my words or actions?

If "yes," why?

Has it caused me or others harm?

If "yes," how can I change?

# Responsibility

> *"The price for greatness is responsibility."*
> *- Winston Churchill*

Although sometimes used interchangeably with accountability, which assigns individual ownership, is results-focused, and generally referred to in past tense, *"responsibility" is usually task-oriented, ongoing, and can be shareable,* like working towards a common goal.

As per Dictionary.com and ChatGPT, *responsibility* refers to the duty or obligation to care for something within one's control. It involves recognizing the impact of your decisions and behavior on others and the environment. Responsibilities can vary based on roles—like being a student, employee, or family member—and often include fulfilling tasks, meeting commitments, and making ethical choices. Being responsible means being reliable and trustworthy in various aspects of life.[1]

Like abdicating accountability, when we abandon responsibilities, overlook, make poor efforts or decisions, repeat mistakes, cheat, or lie, we sabotage our chances for success: a senseless, self-inflicted loss. Remember, *"self-defeating responses are the tools of the incompetent."*

Winners know that assuming responsibility is an empowering building block for achieving and accomplishing individual and collaborative goals. There is *"no"* victory without it. They recognize clearly defined responsibilities and unwavering dedication as *essential* contributors to a triumphant life.

"Assume responsability;
faulting others is the water
in which dreams and
relationships
drown."

– HCJ

# *Insignificant Task?*

The day when the jobs were handed out was one of the most exciting for all the children in the class. It took place during the first week of the term. On that day, every boy and girl was given a job for which they would be responsible for the rest of that school year.

As with everything, some jobs were more interesting than others, and the children were eager to be given one of the best ones. When giving them out, the teacher considered which pupils had been most responsible during the previous year, and those children were the ones who most looked forward to this day.

Among them, Rita stood out. She was a kind and quiet girl, and during the previous year, she had carried out the teacher's instructions perfectly. All the children knew Rita was the favorite to be given the best job of all: to look after the class dog.

But that year, there was a big surprise. Each child received one of the regular jobs, like preparing the books or the radio for the lessons, telling the time, cleaning the blackboard, or looking after one of the pets. But Rita's job was very different.

She was given a little box containing some sand and one ant. And even though the teacher insisted that this ant was very special, Rita could not help feeling disappointed.

Most of her classmates felt sorry for her. They sympathized with her and remarked on how unfair it was that she had been given that job. Even her father became very angry with the teacher, and, as an act of protest, he encouraged Rita to pay no attention to this insignificant pet. However, Rita, who liked her teacher very much, preferred to show the teacher her error by doing something special with that job of such little interest.

*"I will turn this little task into something great,"* Rita told herself.

So it was that Rita started investigating all about her little ant. She learned about the different species and studied everything about their habitats and behavior. She modified the little box to make it perfect for the ant. Rita gave the ant the very best food, and it ended up growing quite a bit bigger than anyone had expected.

One day in spring, when they were in the classroom, the door opened, revealing a man who looked rather

173

important. The teacher interrupted the class with great joy and said, *"This is Doctor Martinez. He has come to tell us a wonderful piece of news, isn't that right?"*

*"Exactly,"* said the doctor. *"Today, they have published the results of the competition, and this class has been chosen to accompany me this summer on a journey to the tropical rainforest, where we will be investigating all kinds of insects. Among all the schools of this region, without a doubt it is this one which has best cared for the delicate little ant given to you. Congratulations! You will be wonderful assistants!"*

That day, the school was filled with joy and celebration. Everyone congratulated the teacher for thinking of entering them into the competition, and they thanked Rita for having been so patient and responsible.

And so it was that many children learned that to be given the most important tasks, *you have to know how to be responsible even in what are apparently the smallest tasks.*

And without doubt, it was Rita who was most pleased with this, having said to herself so many times, *"I will turn this little job into something really great."*

https://www.parthsawhney.com/a-short-story-about-taking-responsibility/ Story by Pedro Pablo Sacristán

**Things to Ponder!**

Whether at home with our loved ones, at play, at work, or within social interaction, we must do our tasks carefully and diligently as it sets a favorable tone for our accomplishments and triumphs. *No task is too small or insignificant.* There is always a hidden or plain purpose behind it.

If we want to succeed, we must be *"responsible"* and commit to seeing all tasks through to the best of our abilities. There is an old Zen saying: *The way a person does one thing is the way they do everything.* Make responsibility the backbone of your actions, and it will bring you joy, peace, and success.

How do I demonstrate that I am a responsible individual?

# Commitment

> "*Commitment is what transforms a promise into reality.*"
> – *Abraham Lincoln*

Conceptually, "<u>*commitment*</u>" refers to the obligation or dedication to a course of action. It manifests in relationships, work, goals, professions, visions, academic pursuits, and community.

*Commitment* involves staying loyal and persevering through obstacles and challenges.

It requires long-term devotion, mutual support, understanding, effort, dedication, time, and resources. People who commit and follow through are viewed as reliable and trustworthy.[1]

Whether liked or disliked, applying commitment and diligence to our undertakings is a mandatory combustible for the prosperous realization of our life's journey.

*Where there is no commitment, there is zero progress.*

With so much at stake, why do so many stay on the sidelines and not commit? Is it that they are scared to make a mistake or waiting for a better opportunity, better time, or a sure thing? *Life offers us no guarantees.* We can either commit and participate and reap its rewards or renegade ourselves to failure, poverty, and unhappiness as we watch our lives pass us by, like on a movie screen.

*"Commitment*
*is the foundation of*
*great accomplishments."*
– Heidi Reeder

## *Claudia Miclaus - A Story About Commitment*

There was a moment in my life when I had to have four jobs at once. Yes, 4! It happened in France. I barely had enough time to run from one place to another, not even mentioning anything about sleep or rest.

What kept me going was, to an extent, survival and building my business. *But most of all, it was commitment.* I could see what was possible; it was so clear in my mind. I envisioned it, and I still see it. And my biggest hope for every one of us is to see it.

How committed are you to show up and go for it? To do whatever you have to do? No matter how it makes you look... small, bad, foolish, not there yet, or many other versions of "not ready" or "not good enough."

*At that moment, I understood that what I do is not who I am. It gave me power. I understood that I was invaluable simply existing and being alive, and I didn't need a fancy title to be a validated human being. Such a game-changer!*

Holy F! I felt like I won the game of life. I was free to do anything. It felt like I escaped from prison.

So, stay on the rollercoaster until the ride ends. Great things need time to manifest; be patient with your journey!

https://claudiamiclaus.com/a-short-story-about-commitment/

**Things to Ponder!**

We all make contributions throughout our lives, but *"commitments"* differ. Like in the analogy of the Chicken and the Pig, in which the chicken is contributing her eggs for breakfast, while the pig is committed to providing the bacon, the moral is whether we are just involved in our life projects or truly commited.

No one has ever said that success is easy. But it's rewarding, empowering, and life-changing. Claudia Miclaus's story is a quintessential example of commitment, accomplishment, never giving up, and, in the process, finding who you are.

Most of us have the wherewithal to reach great heights. As Claudia pointed out, we must *"envision it, see it,"* and then steadfastly go for it. There is no room for meager, half-hearted efforts, as living so forfeits our inherent worth.

Do I commit to living my best life?

If "yes," how?

If "no," why not?

How can I change my lack of commitment?

# Competitiveness, Success & Excellence

> *"Look in the mirror. That's your competition."*
> *- Unknown*

The desire to excel and compete refers to the ability to perform and achieve objectives and goals.[1]

Within our lives, being *"competitive"* implies that we constantly measure ourselves against others. Early in life, we are taught by our loved ones, culture, schools, society, organizations, and country that if we are to succeed, we must engage in endless competition against everyone and everything.

Intellectually and in school, we are informed that those with the best grades will have an advantage. Physically and in sports, the fittest are sought. Emotionally, we should be agreeable, joyous, and stable. Socially, we are to be liked, the life of the party. Lastly, we are to be financially well-off and secure our share of resources. This is the essence of competition and success. *Is it?*

For many, our learned competitive behavior often leaves us living a life where we are always reaching, desiring, and

183

striving but never *enjoying* the journey, even when reaching the objectives or goals.

*"Competition is crucial for our individual and collective growth."* And a slight change in the interpretation of its gist can free us from the demands and burdens we have grown to live with. The understanding is simple but highly rewarding.

*The competition we are to engage in is with ourselves, with the collaboration of all.* The *focus and by-product* become the same: healthy, fulfilling competition, objectives, goals, and relationships beneficial to us all.

*"Your opponent is not your competition. It's your level of preparedness, effort and desire."*

\- HCJ

# The Hare and the Tortoise Race

Once upon a time, a tortoise and a hare had an argument about who was faster. They decided to settle the argument with a race. They agreed on a route and started off the race.

The hare shot ahead and ran briskly for some time. Then, seeing that he was far ahead of the tortoise, he thought he'd sit under a tree for some time and relax before continuing the race. He sat under the tree and soon fell asleep. The tortoise plodding on overtook him and soon finished the race, emerging as the undisputed champ. The hare woke up and realized that he'd lost the race.

*The moral* - Slow and steady wins the race.

## *The Story Doesn't End Here*

The hare was disappointed at losing the race and did some soul-searching. He realized he'd lost the race only because he had been overconfident, careless, and lax. If he had not taken things for granted, there's no way the tortoise could have beaten him. So, he challenged the tortoise to another race. The tortoise agreed. This time, the hare went all out and ran without stopping from start to finish. He won by several miles.

*The moral* – Fast and consistent will always beat the slow and steady. It's good to be slow and steady, but it's better to be fast and reliable.

## The Story Continues

The tortoise did some thinking this time and realized there was no way it could beat the hare in a race the way it was currently formatted. It thought for a while and then challenged the hare to another race but on a slightly different route. The hare agreed.

They started off. In keeping with his self-made *commitment* to be consistently fast, the hare took off and ran at top speed until he came to a broad river. The finishing line was a couple of kilometers on the other side of the river. The hare sat there wondering what to do. In the meantime, the tortoise trundled along, got into the river, swam to the opposite bank, continued walking, and finished the race.

*The moral* – First, identify your core competency and then change the playing field to suit your core competency.

## The Story Still Hasn't Ended

By this time, the hare and the tortoise had become pretty good friends, and they did some thinking together. Both realized that the last race could have been run much better. So they decided to do the last race again, but to run as a team this time.

They started off, and this time, the hare carried the tortoise to the riverbank. There, the tortoise took over and swam across with the hare on his back. On the opposite bank, the hare again carried the tortoise, and they reached the finishing line together. They both felt a greater sense of satisfaction than they'd felt earlier.

*The moral* – It's good to be individually brilliant and to have strong core competencies, but unless you're able to work in a team and harness each other's core competencies, you'll always perform below par because there will always be situations at which you'll do poorly and someone else does well."

https://www.linkedin.com/pulse/very-interesting-read-hare-tortoise-race-complete-story-imran-ali/ Imran Ali May 22, 2017

## Things to Ponder!

When faced with failure, sometimes it is appropriate to work harder and put in more effort. Sometimes, it is reasonable to change strategy and try something else. At times, it is essential to do both.

The story of "The Hare and the Tortoise Race" also shares that *"We perform far better when we stop competing against a rival and instead start competing against the situation."*

Individuals and groups who excel know that the *"competition"* is always about becoming their best version and helping others do the same.

How am I competitive?

Am I competitive to a point that is detrimental to myself or others?

Do I adjust my strategy if need be?

# Success

> *"Success is the sum of small efforts, repeated day in and day out."*
> - Robert Collier

Within our American society, "*success*" is usually referred to or attributed to those who have reached a high level of financial, educational, professional, or material independence.

Even though we can aspire to society's interpretation of success, we must be mindful of the potential pitfalls. And that we can only be content and truly achieve when we subscribe to living an emotionally balanced and empowered life.

*Success without peace and happiness is meaningless.*

No matter what we choose our life's journey to be, we can ensure its integral success by first nurturing our being. That is feeding that yearning for incorporeal growth and unconditionally sharing our love, time, talent, and treasures.

Short—and long-term success is a daily commitment to personal and relational growth. No man is a self-sufficient island. We will encounter personal obstacles, challenging relationships, and environments. How we perceive, react to, and process these problems will be crucial for our success.

During difficult times, people and situations are a *portal* for our growth. Great times are fun, but little, if nothing, is garnered from them. Learn to view your challenges as opportunities for improvement, and your path and commitment to success will become easier.

It is essential to note that success is subjective, and its implied meaning can vary between individuals, groups, cultures, and organizations, depending on values, perspectives, objectives, and goals.

For some individuals, the overwhelming emphasis might be on attaining high status, wealth, and material possessions, even at the expense of all else. At the extreme opposite end of the spectrum, some feel disillusioned, burdened, or even paralyzed by the incessant self-imposed or societal demands to have and live a "successful life." Either way, we are left unhappy.

Living and being successful is not about this. As previously mentioned, having personal, relational, and spiritual growth and balance empowers our physical and emotional well-being, fulfillment, happiness, and goals.

As per Dictionary.com and AI, success is the favorable accomplishment of one's goals or endeavors. *It is aligning one's actions and values with one's intentions.* It is a journey, not a destination. A continuous process of striving toward improvement, accomplishment, satisfaction, and fulfillment.[1]

*"Action is*
*the foundational key*
*to all success."*
*- Pablo Picasso*

## *Sylvester Stallone*

Sylvester Stallone has one of the most inspiring success stories. Before he made it big, he was essentially a starving artist. For many years during and after his college years, he worked odd jobs to pay the bills. He would do so while simultaneously taking on any acting roles he could find to keep his dreams of becoming a successful actor alive.

It was a struggle that Stallone would endure for many years, seven in fact. Throughout those seven challenging years, he would gain a few minor roles in a handful of movies. But none of them were grand enough to get his career launched.

During those seven long years of striving, he came face-to-face with near poverty. Stallone was so desperate for money that, at one point, he had to sell his wife's jewelry. He even had to sell his dog because he couldn't keep him fed. Things got so bad that he even had to endure homelessness for a short period of time.

But, his days of struggle as an aspiring actor would not last forever.

After facing seemingly insurmountable odds for over seven years, he would finally get his big break. And this break would come after he managed to get a script he wrote in a three-day flurry of inspiration in front of two big-shot directors in Hollywood. It was this defining moment that would turn the tide for Sylvester Stallone. And his career would skyrocket after he negotiated the lead role in the film that would come to be known as "Rocky."

https://thestrive.co/inspirational-success-stories/

## Things to Ponder!

The road to *"success"* is often paved with suffering, hardship, and turmoil.

What difficulties have I experienced on my path to success?

"*Success is not final,*
*and failure is seldom fatal.*
*It will be our desire and diligence*
*that will empower us to*
*greater heights.*"

- *HCJ*

# Oprah Winfrey

Oprah Winfrey's success story is very unique. From a very early age, she experienced a level of adversity and poverty that most people would struggle to overcome. She was born into poverty and a broken home in rural Mississippi. Her parents, who were just 18 and 19 when they had her, split soon after she was born. This lead to her being taken in by her grand mother.

Her grandmother was not your typical warm and fuzzy grandmother. No, she was a hard-nosed grandmother who was an extreme disciplinarian who disciplined her for even the slightest offenses. But, the poverty and disciplined lifestyle didn't last forever as she moved back with her mother at the age of six.

Oprah would then experience sexual assault at an early age, having been molested as early as 9 by some of her family members. Having been emotionally abandoned, abused, and molested, she eventually started part-taking in extremely risky behaviors. Behaviors which eventually led to her becoming pregnant at the age of 14.

Then, because she got pregnant, her mother kicked her out of the house. Oprah would go on to live with her father, only to then lose the baby a week after he was born.

Needless to say, Oprah's early life was chockful of struggle, adversity, and tragedy. But, regardless of all of her unfortunate experiences, she decided to turn her life around after she lost her baby. *So, she committed herself to getting an education, becoming her best, and going after her dreams.*

*She decided to start trusting herself again, loving herself, and making choices that would improve her life versus destroy it.* One day, she garnered enough confidence to participate in a beauty pageant. And it was her participation in this pageant that would eventually lead her to a job working for a radio station doing the news.

Oprah's love for speaking to an audience set the stage for continued success as she would go on to become a news anchor. She would eventually leverage this to host a TV chat show in Maryland, ultimately leading to her morning talk show in Chicago.

And as they say, the rest was history. Oprah overcame massive challenges in her youth. Challenges that side line all too many people. She chose to turn her wounds into wisdom and went on to become one of the most successful talk show hosts in history (by helping many others do the same) with her own self-named talk show, The Oprah Winfrey Show. Oprah is now one of the wealthiest self-made women in America.

https://thestrive.co/inspirational-success-stories/

**Things to Ponder!**

Although people can view and define personal, societal, and organizational success differently, they adhere to a common denominator. *"Successful" individuals use challenges and difficulties not as an excuse for failure but as fuel that empowers them to grow, achieve, and prosper.*

Finally, the simplest definition of success is being content and happy wherever you are in life.

Do challenges and difficulties overwhelm me?
If "yes," how can I overcome this?
How can I become successful?

# Excellence

> *"Excellence is never an accident.*
> *It is always the result of high intention,*
> *sincere effort, and intelligent execution."*
> *- Aristotle*

I purposefully share and write about *"excellence"* and not perfection here because the latter is nearly impossible to achieve and requires a one hundred percent achievement or success measure throughout our undertakings.

Early in my college days, I realized that my predisposition toward life was that of a perfectionist. Unlike what I knew, and many may think, this was not an asset but a hindrance and detriment to my future undertakings and aspirations.

Fortunately, life would intervene. One day, while conversing with an individual I had never met nor would ever encounter again, I shared my bias on living a life striving for perfection.

He suggested that reaching for *excellence* during our lifetime was a preferable approach to living. That perfection was an all-consuming, often unreachable aspiration, at times leaving one exhausted, dissatisfied, or feeling like a failure. He shared with me that a conviction towards excellence afforded us the opportunity for a happy, satisfying, less consuming, and demanding life while working to do and be our best.

I would take the advice to heart and dedicate my life to excellence. This change in viewpoint has had a significant impact on my life. It has given me the awareness, openness, and ability to accept far less than once required results as splendidly fine building blocks. It has also taught me that failures only exist when we choose not to learn from, overcome, or adapt to challenges.

*Excellence* addresses the quality of being exceptional in our endeavors. It is a standard of achievement that results in a culture of outstanding skill, performance, distinction, and high success. It requires commitment, dedication, and the pursuit of reaching for one's full potential. It is an applicable guiding principle that leads to success in all facets of individual, social, and organizational life.[1]

*"Excellence
is not an end, but
a journey of continuous
improvement."*
– *Unknown*

# The Sculptor

A German once visited a temple under construction where he saw a sculptor making an idol of God. Suddenly, he saw a similar idol lying nearby. Surprised, he asked the sculptor, *"Do you need two statues of the same idol?"*

*"No,"* said the sculptor without looking up. *"We need only one, but the first one got damaged at the last stage."* The gentleman examined the idol but did not find any apparent damage. *"Where is the damage?"* he asked.

*"There is a scratch on the nose of the idol,"* said the sculptor, still busy with his work. *"Where are you going to install the idol?"*

The sculptor replied that *"it would be installed on a pillar 20 feet high."*

*"If the idol is that far up, who is going to know that there is a scratch on the nose?"* the gentleman asked.

The sculptor stopped his work, looked up at the gentleman, smiled, and said, *"I will know it!"*

https://steemit.com/life/@sharananurag998/an-inspirational-short-story-on-excellence

**Things to Ponder!**

The ancient Greeks believed that happiness is the end goal of life in the sense of well-being, resulting from achieving *"excellence"* in fulfilling one's function.

Excellence is a personal motivator. It is not for someone else but for your accomplishment, satisfaction, and reward. Don't climb mountains so the world can see you, but climb the hills to see the world.

As Oprah Winfrey shared: *"Let excellence be your brand. When you are excellent, you become unforgettable!"*

Am I a perfectionist?

　If "yes," how does the striving for perfection make me feel?

　Can I benefit from pursuing excellence instead?

　How would I feel?

# Self-Confidence & Self-Worth

> *"No one can make you feel inferior without your consent."*
> *- Eleanor Roosevelt*

Many spend a lifetime questioning their *"self-confidence and self-worth"* without realizing that for most, feeling positive and deserving about ourselves, or the lack thereof, starts early in our childhood when we are either praised for our good works or demeaned for ill-advised, non-conforming responses and actions by our parents, teachers or societal norms and rules.

Regarding life's adversities and struggles, we can blame our past adverse exposures for our current challenging times or awaken to the reality that we can change this. As adults, most of us have the emotional or intellectual resources we did not possess as children to stop victimizing our lives.

Specifically, *self-confidence* is a belief in oneself and one's powers, abilities, and judgment. *Self-worth*, or self-esteem, refers to the intrinsic sense or perception of one's value, worth as a person, self-respect, ability, and surety.[1]

The approach to building up our confidence and worth is twofold. We must first let go of past-related detrimental thoughts that derail our present and future responses and actions.

This is primarily accomplished through introspection and reflection on our previous negative encounters, learning the harm they caused us, assuming personal responsibility wherever required, and forgiving ourselves and others for our pain and loss.

Secondly, we must realize that through our past efforts, confidence, and worth, we have experienced success, i.e., graduating elementary school, high school, college, trade school, holding a job, marriage, etc., and that an added cure for lacking self-confidence and self-worth is addressing our intellectual, emotional and spiritual ailments through counseling, education, emulating previous positive actions, and the actions of successful role models.

"Self-Confidence is a super power. Once you start to believe in yourself; magic starts happening."

- Unknown

## *An Old Watch and Self-Worth*

Before he died, a father told his son, *"Here is a watch your grandfather gave me... It is almost 200 years old. Before I give it to you, go to the jewelry store in the city. Tell them I want to sell it and see how much they offer you."*

The son went to the jewelry store, came back to his father, and said, *"They offered $100 because it is so old."* The father said, *"Well, try the pawnshop."*

The son went to the pawnshop, returned to his father, and said, *"The pawnshop offered only $20 because it has a scratch."* The father asked his son to go to the museum and show them the watch.

The son quietly questioned his father's judgment but went to the museum, willing to act on his last wishes. When he came back, he said to his father, *"The curator offered $375,000 for this very rare piece to be included in their precious antique collection."*

The father responded, *"I wanted to show you that the right place will value you in the right way. Don't find yourself in the wrong place and get angry because you are not valued. Never stay in a place where someone doesn't see your value, or you don't feel appreciated.*"If you don't know your value, you will always settle for far less than you deserve.

*"People who don't know their value settle for less than they are worth in relationships. When it comes to their profession, job, or friendships, they know they are worth more, but they settle for someone else's definition of their worth."*

You see, that is the difference between most people and the few. That is the difference between people who love the life they have created for themselves and those who can't stand the life they are living. *"You Have To Know Your Worth!"*

*"Most people will allow just about anyone to influence their perception of themselves. But people who love their life refuse to accept the opinions of small-minded people."*

They refuse to be put in a box. They will not be defined by anyone but themselves. They know their value is set by themselves, their thoughts about who they are, not someone else's opinion of what they are worth.

*"Don't let them put a price on you! You set your own price! And don't give discounts to other people so you can fit in or be liked. People pleasers never end up*

*happy in the end. Put yourself first."*

You must build your self-worth by the work you do every day on yourself. You build it by the way that you show up every single day. Day in and day out, no excuses, no shortcuts, just a relentless dedication to be the best you can be.

If you have someone in your life who tries to diminish your abilities in any way, the time has come to move those people along. It's time to awaken that part of you that demands more for your life. Because only you know what you are truly capable of. It's time to wake up and shock the world!

*"Shock those that doubted you with a disturbing level of determination. Shock those who doubted you with a commitment to excellence that those with weak hearts cannot match. Shock those who doubted you with your actions today as you draw a line in the sand and commit to becoming the person no one thought you could be."* Because only you know what you are truly capable of.

In this world, you only have to earn the respect of one person; that person is you. You determine the level you demand of yourself.

It's time to demand more! It's time to prove, once and for all, who you are. Who you will become! And what you will never settle for again. Raise your standards. Rise to a higher level, and let no one question your integrity again.

*"Day by day. Brick by brick. You start now. You build the foundations through the self-work you put in every single day. Build yourself up to become an unbreakable force, an unstoppable machine fueled by the results you get from the work you put in today and every day, from this day until your last."*

No more will you settle for the opinions of others. No more will you compromise for someone else's opinion of your value. Now, you determine your value through self-work, self-education, and self-determination. Your destiny is strictly in your hands.

*"Your pride grows stronger every day from the work You put in!"* You know what you have to do! The time for change is now! Today is the day.

When it comes to your own *Self-Worth, "there is no tomorrow."* Know your worth, and *"Never, Ever settle for anything less!"*

https://www.fearlessmotivation.com/2020/07/16/the-inspiring-story-of-an-old-watch-and-self-worth/ Know Your Worth – Copyright: Fearless Motivation

**Things to Ponder!**

"An Old Watch and Self-Worth" points out the harm of not knowing or allowing others to determine your worth.

Empowered individuals posses a healthy level of *"self-confidence and self-worth."* They are not deterred or persuaded by discerning arguments, comments, or opinions. They know that information, diligence, and optimism are vital to reaching their aspirations and goals. So, they used education, previous favorable performances, proven building blocks, and thriving peers and mentors to fuel their actions.

Do I lack confidence, self-esteem, or self-worth?

If "yes," why?

How can I overcome this?

# Honor, Truth & Your Word

> Honor!
>
> "A veteran, whether active duty, reserve, discharged, retired, living or deceased – from all branches of the Armed Forces, who at one point in their life, wrote a blank check made payable to "The United States of America" for an amount of "Up to, and including their life."
>
> - Nicola Barella

*"Honor, truth, and your word"* are *uncompromising convictions* rooted within the conscience and lives of successful people, relations, and endeavors. Nonetheless, there are some who choose to disregard or forfeit these virtues.

Sacrificing our honor, truth, or word is akin to choosing to fail, for it leaves deep within our core an uncomforting distaste that not only permeates and blemishes our essence but also devalues our character and reputation with others. *"Nothing is ever worth losing that much."*

Hence, when confronted with compromising yourself with less than desirable choices, options, or opportunities, be patient and pass on these, as something better will come along.

As per the Internet and AI, honor, truth, and keeping one's word are equivalent to relying on a person's righteousness, forthrightness, and uncompromising surety.

Explicitly, *honor* is a concept that encompasses a strong sense of integrity, respect, and ethical behavior. It involves adhering to a code of conduct that upholds principles of dignity, fairness, and moral excellence. It often consists of doing what is right, even when difficult, inconvenient, or dangerous, through courage, loyalty, and respect for oneself and others.

*Truth* refers to the state or quality of following fact or reality. It is the concept of being accurate, genuine, and not distorted or misrepresented.

Lastly, keeping *your word* is a crucial aspect of truth and honor. It involves making promises or commitments and following through on them, regardless of the circumstances.[1]

*"Honor is
simply the morality
of superior men."*

\- H.L. Mencken

## *Honor Wins*

In 1959, a young boy named Clifton Davis was on a school trip from New York to Washington, D.C., with his eighth-grade classmates. As part of the trip, they were scheduled to visit an amusement park in Maryland.

The morning after the school group toured our nation's monuments to freedom and equality, the school chaperones learned that the amusement park was for whites only (this was in the not-so-far distant past when such egregious bigotry was common in America). Clifton was black, and when they explained this to him, he returned to his hotel room in tears.

When young Clifton told his classmates he would have to stay behind at the hotel, his friend Frank Miller did not hesitate. He immediately declared that he would not go either. Then, he told other kids in the group what was happening to Clifton. Soon, Clifton's room was filled with kids, and before he knew it, eleven young men decided they would rather support their friend than go to an amusement park practicing such discrimination.

Years later, in 1991, Mr. Davis sat in a meeting listening to a young man named Dondré Green tell of attending a high school golf tournament at a private club in Louisiana.

When the team walked out onto the course, club officials told the coach that because Dondré was black, he could not play with his team. There was no debate when the coach pulled the seniors aside to tell them this. The seniors knew what was right and wrong and what was of secondary importance. They turned and walked off the course with the younger players following their example.

https://user.xmission.com/~wake/honor Compiled by Paul Wake

## Things to Ponder!

We are perceptible beings who can easily spot inequity, injustice, and unfair action and treatment. *"Honor Wins"* speaks about young men who understood that honor and integrity should never be forfeited for tainted gains, rewards, or trophies.

Am I honorable with decisions and choices, or do I cave in?

If I fail to live honorably, why? How do I feel?

Am I willing to change?

"If you tell
the truth, you don't
have to remember anything."
- Mark Twain

## *The Naked Truth and The Lie*

I often find myself fascinated with the intricacies of how we perceive the truth and how we are willing to accept it or reject it to give ourselves peace of mind when confronted with inconvenient realities.

It seems we as a society have become experts (whether it be consciously or subconsciously) in deconstructing what we know are factual truths and then reconstructing them to be more appropriate, more righteous, and even more politically correct.

We perform mental gymnastics, accepting certain aspects of a factual reality while omitting or outright rejecting other elements of that same reality in order to drive home a point we want to make.

Why do we do this? Why have we become so good at it? A stranger recently told me a story which seemed to make the answer to these questions quite clear. The story goes something like this:

One day, a man named Truth and a man named Lie stood by a river just outside of town. They were twin brothers.

Lie challenged Truth to a race, claiming he could swim across the river faster than Truth. Lie laid out the rules to the challenge, stating that they both must remove all their clothes and, at the count of 3, dive into the freezing cold water and swim to the other side and back.

Lie counted to 3, but when Truth jumped in, Lie did not. As Truth swam across the river, Lie put on Truth's clothes and walked back to town dressed as Truth. He proudly paraded around town pretending to be Truth.

Truth made it back to shore, but his clothes were gone, and he was left naked with only Lie's clothes to wear. Refusing to dress himself as Lie, Truth walked back to town naked.

People stared and glared as naked Truth walked through town. He tried to explain what happened and that he was, in fact, Truth, but because he was naked and uncomfortable to look at, people mocked and shunned him, refusing to believe he was really Truth. The people in town chose to believe Lie because he was dressed appropriately and easier to look at.

From that day until now, people have come to *believe* a lie rather than a naked truth.

https://medium.com/@ParkerSimpson/the-story-of-truth-lie-1476bda2d45e - Parker Simpson

## Things to Ponder!

There are no replacements for the truth. *A "truth" is always quantifiable, empowering, and eternal.* A lie is always deceiving, compromising, and usually detrimental in some shape or form.

The story of the two brothers, "Truth" and "Lie," reminds us not to fall for the shortcomings that deception comes disguised as.

How "The Naked Truth and The Lie" applies to modern-day society is that we often consciously or subconsciously *reject* truths for temporary relief, rewards, to save face, or false peace of mind. Sometimes at our peril.

Our country is no different. It is divided among ideological lines on every front. People can be presented with irrefutable evidence regarding governing, global warming, terrorism, societal issues like race relations, cultural differences, and countless other problems, but many still evade the truth and decide instead to believe the well-dressed lie, especially when it's beneficial to their idealistic narrative or agenda.

In the end, one must be vigilant against deception since, whether aware of it or not, there is a toll paid for propagating or believing falsehoods.

Have I been a victim of deception in the past?

    If "yes," how did I feel?

Do I deceive myself or others?

    If I do, why?

    How can I stop lying to myself and misleading others?

"When you
don't keep your word,
you lose credibility."
- Robin Sharma

## *Keeping Your Word*

Several months ago, a former executive at our company made a commitment to a third party via email.

It is obvious that he didn't research the cost of his promise, nor did he get anyone else's approval. I was not aware of the obligation until the other party brought it to our attention. When I learned that the commitment was north of six figures, I gasped.

Several rationalizations immediately popped into my head:

The executive is no longer at the company.
He obviously didn't count the cost.
He wasn't authorized to make this commitment.
This project is already under water.
This amount is not in our budget.
I wasn't even aware of the commitment.
Our CFO wasn't aware of the commitment.

However, after a few moments, I remembered that our first core value at Thomas Nelson is *"Honoring God."* We amplify this by saying, "*We honor God in everything we do.*" We then go on to describe the behaviors that express this value. The fourth item on the list is this: "We honor our commitments, even when it is difficult, expensive, or inconvenient."

That brought everything into clear focus. This was initially motivated by Psalm 15:1,4: LORD, who may abide in Your tabernacle? Who may dwell in Your holy hill? He who swears to his own hurt and does not change.

Simply put, this means that *"our word is sacred."* I don't think it is claiming too much to say that this premise is the foundation of Western society. Without it, our society begins to fall apart.

When I was growing up, a promise and a handshake were all you needed. Contracts were largely foreign and unnecessary. In fact, to insist on one would have been an insult. Why? Because a man's word was his bond. No one was willing to risk their social capital or relational equity by breaking their word.

My, how times have changed. Twice in the last month, I have had people blatantly dishonor their word. Both were under contract. Their obligations were explicit. There was no ambiguity.

This is tragic—especially for them. <u>*"Keeping your word* is the essence of *integrity."*</u>

As Stephen Covey points out, *"honesty is making your words conform to reality. Integrity is making reality conform to your words."* It is essential to our success and leadership. Without it, winning is short-lived and worthless.

Why? *"Integrity is required for trust."* If people can't trust your word, they won't trust you. *"Trust is necessary for influence."* People *"choose"* those they let influence them, and this is based largely on trust.

*"Influence is essential for impact."* You can't make the impact you want to make unless you can influence others and shift their behavior.

https://fullfocus.co/keeping-your-word/  Michael Hyatt -Mansi
SharmaMittal (Momspresso.com)

**Things to Ponder!**

Keeping *"your word"* is sometimes complicated, expensive, and inconvenient. But then, what are we if not our word? A failed commitment, a broken promise, a lost trust.

In a considerably fragile world, trust is expensive and rare. But the price of not doing so is even *more damaging*. It will ultimately cost your reputation, success, and peace of mind.

Do I always keep my word?

If "yes," how?

If "no," how does this make me feel?

Is there ever an advantage or reward for not keeping my word?

Has someone not honored their word to me?

If yes, what impact did it have on me?

How did I feel?

# Patience

> "To lose patience is to lose the battle."
> – Mahatma Gandhi

One of the best virtues in life is *"patience."* It's the disposition to allow time to share with loved ones, colleagues, and strangers as well as reflect and perhaps come up with a clearer perspective, alternate point of view, or calmer response to an issue or problem at hand.

*Patience* is a learnable skill that allows one to collaborate more effectively. It helps prevent hasty, selfish decisions, irritable and defensive responses, discontent, and frustration. It enables us to grow in self-control, focus, resiliency, perseverance, tolerance, humility, generosity, empathy for others' plight, and better responses to our aspirations and purpose.[1]

Unfortunately, far too many of us are complicit in living a rushed life and often engage in impulsive, poorly thought-out decisions or responses to life's questions, trials, and tribulations.

## The Essence of Winners - *Patience*

We must learn to be present in our daily journey and be sure that we are not acting as reactive individuals but as alert and proactive people living life from a paradigm based on the awareness and implications of our actions, choices, responses, and discernment of information.

*Ultimately, patience is about improving one's quality of life and odds of success and providing us with a harmonious, fulfilling life. The choice is simple: thrive with patience or live an agitated, ungrounded existence!*

*"One minute of patience,*

*ten years of peace."*

– Anonymous

## *Precious Encounter*

A New York City taxi driver arrives at the final stop for his shift. He honked. After waiting a few minutes, he honked again. Because it was his last stop, he considered pulling away. Instead, he parked the car and walked up to the door.

He knocked.
He heard an elderly voice, *"Just a minute."*
He then heard the shuffling of bags moving across the floor. Then the door opened.

It was a small woman in her 90s with a soft smile wearing a print dress and a pillbox hat with a veil pinned on it. As she answered, the taxi driver caught a glimpse inside the house. It looked as if no one had lived there for years. All the furniture was covered in sheets, no clocks on the wall and no knickknacks on the counters.

*"Could you carry my bag?"* the lady asked.
The cab driver walked her slowly down the front porch steps to the cab.

Once in the cab, the lady handed the driver an address and asked, *"Could you drive through downtown?*

*"It's not the shortest way,"* The driver answered.

*"I'm in no hurry. I don't mind,"* she said. *"I'm on my way to hospice…"*

The driver and passenger shared a quick glimpse in the rearview mirror, enough for her to see his concern and continue, *"I don't have any family left. The doctor says I don't have very long."*

The driver quietly reached over and shut off the meter, then asked,

*"What route would you like me to take?"* For the next two hours, they drove through the city.

She showed the driver where she once worked, the neighborhood where she and her husband first lived, a furniture warehouse that had once been a ballroom when she was a girl. There were a few parts of town she asked the driver to slow down, and she would sit, staring into the darkness, saying nothing.

After a couple of hours, she suddenly said, *"I'm tired. Let's go now."*

They drove in silence to the address she had given him. When they arrived, two orderlies came out to the cab as soon as they pulled up. They must have been expecting her.

The driver opened the trunk to take out the suitcase. As he shut the trunk, she was already in a wheelchair. *"How much do I owe you?"* She asked, reaching into her purse.

*"Nothing,"* said the driver.
*"You have to make a living,"* she answered.
*"There are other passengers,"* he responded.

Almost without thinking, the driver bent and gave the lady a hug. She held on tightly.
*"You gave an old woman a little moment of joy,"* she said. *"Thank you."*

The driver squeezed the lady's hand, and the two turned to go their separate ways. As he got in the car and glanced over to her, the door was shut. That night, he could hardly speak.

The taxi driver couldn't shake the feeling that this encounter may have been one of the most important moments of his life.

https://medium.com/@willkrieger/a-story-of-patience-758a4b6704b1
Will Krieger Nov.13, 2018

## Things to Ponder!

*"Patience" is one of the cornerstones of success.* Yet, *within the immediate gratifying environment many are a part of,* it is disregarded as requiring too much time and effort or simply overlooked.

*Life is fleeting and precious, with significant consequences for poor decisions and choices and a lack of fruitful relationships. Unliked our unbridled, instance reward-seeking mind, the cultivation of "patience," knowledge, and wisdom propels us to make diligent, well-informed actions that benefit our collective lives and, most importantly, lead us to have caring, rewarding interactions with others.*

As previously mentioned, *patience* is a learnable skill. One can begin to nurture it at home by spending several moments present (no distractions – cell phones, tablets, TV, etc.) each day with the people in your life.

Listen intently to your spouse, converse with your kids, check up on a neighbor, or pay attention to a coworker's struggle. It could not only mean the world to both of you, but you might learn some valuable lessons.

## The Essence of Winners - *Patience*

As "Precious Encounter" points out, taking time for others is rewarding to all.

Am I impatient with myself and others? If "yes," why?

How does being impatient make me feel?

Have I lost opportunities or failed in relationships because of impatience?

## - Living Fundamentals -

### The Essence of Winners

### Living Fundamentals

*"You are not a drop in the ocean.*
*You are the entire ocean in a drop."*

\- Rumi

# Doctrine

> *"The greatest journey you will ever take is the journey to discover yourself."*
> - Deepak Chopra

Much has been said, written, and even fought over God, spirituality, love, and morality - _doctrine_. We will add prose to what role these could play in our path to lasting success.

For those who believe in a supreme being or supernatural force that oversees or guides our lives, the meaning of love and God can be considered synonymous. These terms are associated with all that is good, worthwhile, fulfilling, and caring, leading us to live a harmonious, happy existence.

When we live or speak about the religious, spiritual, and mindful constructs that are conduits to many people's success, the active or participating approach can be quite distinct.

Religious or religion deals with rules, ceremonies, and doctrine used for a uniform approach towards God. Spirituality addresses self-examination, contemplation, empowerment, and return to the incorporeal, our innermost being, our oneness with the divine. The consciousness, presence, and essence that is beyond form and never die, our soul. Mindfulness brings us into the present moment, self-awareness of our thoughts, activities, actions, ramifications, and our identity and wholeness with all.

Our moral code, rules, or principles are derived partly from our upbringing, religion, spiritual affiliation, and mindful presence. As a guiding set of ethical instructions or virtuous conduct, it can evolve and change depending on ethnicity, culture, time, and personal awareness.

An example of such change is that if you were a woman or man living in the States and going to the beach during the 1920s required that your bathing suit cover most of your body. That was the "moral" standard. Today, most of our bodies are exposed, covered by little fabric, or nude if we attend a nudist beach.

Still, in some countries, due to their religious, cultural, or moral standard, women must wear a hijab or burka covering their faces, hair, and bodies and are still not allowed to drive, vote, or get a higher education.

Lastly, mindful awareness enhances our view, ownership, and collaboration with everyone else, every living creature, and our environment because we come to know, value, and respect the essence and vital nature of our interconnectedness and interdependence.

As per internet definitions and AI, GOD is defined as one or more deities presiding over worldly affairs. Love is a feeling of deep affection. Spirituality and mindfulness are divine, metaphysical, and transcendental. Religious – imbued with or exhibiting religion; pious; devout; godly. Morality conforms to the principles or rules of proper ethical or virtuous conduct.[1]

Regardless of your preferred guiding principles or *doctrine,* it is widely accepted that practicing and conforming to sound ethical convictions, religious dogma, and spiritual and mindful precepts can provide a supportive and robust foundation, assisting one to overcome, persevere, and succeed, especially when confronted with hard times or difficult decisions.

"*The privilege of a lifetime is to become who you really are.*"

*- Carl Jung*

# *The Eagle Who Mistook Itself for a Chicken*

A fable is told about an eagle who thought it was a chicken. When the eagle was very young, she fell from the safety of her nest. A chicken farmer found the eagle, brought her to the farm, and raised her in a chicken coop. The eagle grew up believing she was a chicken.

A naturalist came to the chicken farm to see if what he had heard about an eagle acting like a chicken was true. The farmer explained to the naturalist that the bird was no longer an eagle. She was now a chicken because she had been trained to be a chicken and believed she was a chicken.

The naturalist knew that the bird was born an eagle and had the heart of an eagle, and nothing could change that. The man lifted the eagle onto the chicken coop fence and told her to fly. The eagle glanced down at her home among the chickens in the chicken coop where she was comfortable. She jumped off the fence and continued doing what chickens do.

The naturalist returned the next day and tried again to convince the farmer and the eagle that the eagle was born for something greater. He took the eagle to the farmhouse rooftop and told her to fly. The large bird looked at the man, then again down into the chicken coop. She jumped from the man's arm onto the roof of the farmhouse.

The naturalist asked the farmer to let him try one more time. He would return the next day and prove the bird was an eagle. The farmer said, "*It is a chicken.*" The naturalist returned the next morning to the chicken farm and took the eagle and the farmer to the foot of a high mountain. The man held the eagle on his arm and pointed high into the sky. He said, "*Eagle, you are an eagle! You belong to the sky and not to the earth. Stretch your wings and fly.*"

This time, the eagle stared upward into the bright sun, straightened her body, and stretched her wings. Her wings moved slowly at first, then surely and powerfully. With the mighty screech of an eagle, it flew.

The eagle, by nature, flies high, has excellent vision, and chooses what she wants to eat. However, the chicken is a symbol of that which is limited. It is fearful. It does not fly, and it eats what the other chickens eat.

In the course of our lives, we may meet people who want us to *think like a chicken.* And many of us still *think we are chickens.* Throw grains at our feet, and we are content. But even so, we are still eagles. Nothing can change our essence, our identity.

The farmer was fully aware that he had an eagle, but he wanted to turn it into a chicken. He raised it under special conditions so that it would be a chicken and never an eagle. However, a true leader is able to recognize another leader.

*We hope to encounter a leader who will recognize our inner strength and help us fly – so that we may rediscover ourselves and identify no longer as chickens but as eagles. We all have a hidden eagle that inhabits us. The social environment cannot determine our essence, no matter what the farmer or chicken coop says.*

Ultimately, with or without help, we sore like eagles or live like chickens. The choice is ours.

https://www.cscsisters.org/the-eagle-who-mistook-itself-for-a-chicken/ by Sisters Rosevania de Oliveira Pimentel and Vanessa Cruz Ferreira, CSC, Brazil

## Things to Ponder!

Life bestows us our allotment of what we deem obscure, challenging, deficient, bad, and good. Within that, we often claim to be lost, deprived, unfortunate, and even winners.

## The Essence of Winners - *Doctrine*

The belief of what we are is often rooted in our upbringing, exposures, circumstances, and, specifically, the people we surround ourselves with.

As the story "The Eagle Who Mistook Itself for a Chicken" shares, *we must never forget our essence, one with the absolute.* And that when all seems bleak, inherent within us is the strength, determination, and courage to succeed.

How do I see myself? Do I see myself as lacking, unworthy, or insecure? If so, why? How can I change this?

*"Within us
lives the source
of all."*
- HCJ

# God is in The Ordinary

There once was a king whose greatest desire was to gain absolute power over every square inch of his kingdom. He had succeeded in removing all obstacles to his complete control, except the people still put their ancient God above the king.

The king summoned his three wisest advisors to find a way to put an end to such worship. *"Where,"* asked the king, *"where might the people's God be hidden and made to vanish from their lives and cease challenging my rule?"*

The first advisor suggested hiding the God at the summit of the highest mountain. *"No,"* said the king: *"The people would abandon their homes and climb the highest mountain to search for their God."*

The second advisor proposed hiding the people's God at the bottom of the sea. But the king also rejected the idea. *"He said the people would probe the ocean's depth to find their God."*

Finally, the third wisest advisor, a wrinkled and bent older man, spoke his advice in a hoarse whisper. "*O mighty king,* he said, *hide the people's God somewhere in their everyday lives. They will never find it!*

https://philipchircop.wordpress.com/page/2/ Feb 28, 2021

## Things to Ponder!

Just as the wise man's advice to the king, for many of us today, God lies dormant within.

Why is that?
Do I feel empty inside?    If "yes," why?
What role, if any, can GOD play in my life?

*"Help others on their journey, and you will never lack anything."*

*- HCJ*

# Gandhi's Shoes

As Gandhi stepped aboard a train one day, one of his shoes slipped off and landed on the track. He was unable to retrieve it as the train was moving.

To the amazement of his companions, Gandhi calmly took off his other shoe and threw it back along the track to land close to the first.

Asked by a fellow passenger why he did so, Gandhi smiled.

He replied that the poor man who finds the shoes lying on the track will now have a pair he can use.

https://spiritualgrowthevents.com/gandhis-shoes-spiritual-story/

## Things to Ponder!

No one on Mother "Earth" is one hundred percent knowledgeable or autonomous. As the stories in *"Doctrine"* demonstrate, many of us will often need the aid of others to find, know, and understand the limitless source within us and reach our potential.

The Essence of Winners - *Doctrine*

Where am I when it comes to grasping who I am and my role in life?

Am I primarily a taker or a giver in life?
If I am a taker, how can I change this?

# Faith & Hope

> *"Faith is taking the first step*
> *even when you don't see the whole staircase."*
> *- Martin Luther King, JR.*

Although a standard definition of *"faith"* is to trust or have confidence in someone or something, it is a complex and multifaceted concept that can be understood, practiced, and interpreted in various ways, depending on cultural, religious, philosophical, and personal perspectives. Some view faith as a source of strength, inspiration, and comfort, while others may critique it as a potential source of dogmatism or irrationality.[1]

At its core, faith is based on *belief,* and therefore, its outcomes cannot be one hundred percent guaranteed.

Regardless of our interpretation or perspective on *faith*, for many, it's an essential, optimistic inner voice or guidance that, consciously or not, helps us traverse life irrespective of the situation in our lives or that the outcome of any of our subsequent seconds is unknown.

A couple of examples of how we live based on faith are as follows: without thinking about it, we get in our cars expecting to reach our destination without harm or incident. The same holds when we board a flight. We do these and countless other things relying on our prior successful experience, trust, confidence, and faith. But the outcome is never assured.

Whether agnostic, atheist, or believer, ours is a life based on chance and probability. But without faith and hope, we can become dissolution, rudderless, and unhappy.

*"Seeds of faith
are always within us;
sometimes, it takes a crisis
to nourish and encourage
their growth."*

*- Susan L. Taylor*

## A Man in the Desert

It was a hot day, and the sands were glittering like gold in a desert. Andrew, touring the place, lost his way in the desert. He could not find his way back, and the water in his bottle dried.

He was in desperate search of water. Otherwise, he will die due to dehydration. As he struggled walking in the desert, he saw a small hut in the distance. Initially, he thought it was just an illusion. But he continued walking towards it, and as he reached closer, he realized it was a hut.

He opened the door and found nobody there. It seemed like the place had been abandoned for a long time. He was surprised to see a hand water pump with all connections intact and a pipeline to the ground.

Then he started pumping, and there was no sign of water. He continued his effort and gave up due to exhaustion. He began searching the hut for any other source of water. Then he found a bottle of water hidden in the corner.

He was happy. And when he was about to drink the water, he found a piece of paper attached. It was written in the paper, *"Please use this water to start the*

pump. It works. After you have done, do not forget to
refill the bottle again."

After reading the message in the paper, he went into a
dilemma, *"Will the pump work if I use this water? Is
the pump in good condition? Can I trust the words in
the paper? If it is false, my last water source will be
wasted."*

He paused for a minute, closed his eyes, and prayed.
Then he poured the water from the bottle into the
pump and pumped it.

Soon, he heard a bubbling sound, and water started
pouring out. There was a moment of relief on his face.
He drank the water and filled his bottle. Then he got
refreshed and refilled the bottle from the hut.

He stayed in the hut for some time and looked around.
Then he saw a pencil and a map explaining the
direction to the nearby village from the hut location.

He was happy that his faith in the water pump worked.
Similarly, he believed the map would direct him in the
right direction.
Then he wrote in the paper, *"Have faith. It works,"*
returned the bottle and paper to the exact place where

he took it from, and happily left the hut.

https://winnersstory.com/short-stories-on-faith-1/ Padmakar
Deshpande July 5, 2023

## Things to Ponder!

In our lives, there will be many times when we must rely on *"faith."* Conventional knowledge will not always suffice. Successful individuals know this. They persist with diligence, hope, and faith when things look bleak. In significant part because of their effort and belief, somehow, someway, more often than not, they prevail.

Do I believe in the concept of faith? If "yes," why and how? If "no," why not?

Do I have faith that I will succeed in life? If "yes," why? If "no," why not?

Do I lack faith or give up when the going gets tough? If "yes," why?

# Hope

> *"Hope is being able to see that there is light despite all of the darkness."*
> - Desmond Tutu

Unlike many believe, *"hope"* is not a passive endeavor. And without action, it's worthless. Prepare well and hope for the best. Like a well without water does not quench your thirst, diligence is imperative for hope to have a chance.

Specifically, hope is a powerful, fundamental human emotion and coping mechanism, providing individuals with the strength and resilience to face challenges and uncertainties. It manifests as emotional hope, optimism, and positivity arising from a belief in a better future. There is cognitive hope, the mental process of setting goals, creating plans, and envisioning positive outcomes, and behavioral hope, taking actions and making choices that align with the expectation of a positive outcome.[1]

Once the work has been done, all work and thoughts are released into the universe, the playing field of all possibilities, and allowed to percolate and ferment. Thus, another of life's secrets. *One that winners know and rely on.*

*"To live*
*without hope*
*is to cease to live."*
*- Fyodor Dstoevsky*

## *Son, Father, and The Well*

Once, there was a man who was running a business. He faced severe losses and had to sell his properties and cars to continue running the business.

Seeing the situation, the son asked his father, *"Why are you still running the business when you are at a loss?" "Why don't you shut the business?"*

Father smiled and replied, "My son, life can bring us many challenges and even push us down. But we have to hope that we can overcome any challenges."

Son, <u>*"How can hope help us?"*</u> Father, "Ok, I will show you!"

Father took his son to a big well and asked him to jump. Son, in shock, *"Father, I don't know how to swim, So I cannot jump."* But his father pushed his son to the well and went into a hiding place.

Son struggled and kept on trying to float for close to 5 minutes. Then, when he was about to drown, the father jumped and pulled his son out of the well.

The next day, the father again took his son to the well and asked him to jump again. First, he hesitated, then he jumped into the well. Father again went into hiding.

The boy again struggled to keep floating. Time kept on running. After 15 minutes, the Father pulled his son out of the well. Father asked his son, "Why were you pushing harder than yesterday?".

Son replied, *"Yesterday, I did not know what to do when you pushed me into the well. I feared I would drown. But today, with greater effort and fervor, I hoped that you would come and save me."*

https://winnersstory.com/short-stories-hope-1/

**Things to Ponder!**

Life will expose us to innumerable challenges. Some will be emotional, others cognitive, physical, or behavioral. We *"hope"* we can overcome when faced with strenuous demands or adversity.

But *hope* alone without preparedness and action won't be enough.

Imaging hoping you can <u>save</u> a person experiencing cardiac arrest without any prior knowledge and training on CPR(Coronary Pulmonary Resuscitation) is highly improbable.

Hence, for hope to play a viable role in our life's endeavors, whenever possible, we must acquire knowledge and physical experience about our challenges and take the necessary steps to skew the outcome in our favor.

Do I believe in hope?

    If "yes," how does hope manifest in my life?

    If I do not believe in hope, why not?

# Mercy & Forgiveness

*"God's mercy is fresh and new every morning." "Nothing can make injustice just but mercy."*
*"Keep your eyes open to your mercies. The man who forgets to be thankful has fallen asleep in life."*
- Anonymous

The virtues or character traits of excellence, goodness, and righteousness associated with *"mercy"* allow us to be compassionate, understanding, kind, lenient, tolerant, graceful, benevolent, and sympathetic to our and others' plight.[1]

Having mercy towards ourselves and others is an empowering, endearing quality of good leaders. Specific to all is our innate knowledge that we are not entirely autonomous or self-reliant.

We will experience countless disappointments, heartaches, and failures; therefore, we must be forgiving, kind, and fair with ourselves and others. For *there is no success without the participation of others or if our reward leaves us with a sour taste or uneasy feeling.*

For *those who understand the generous nature of mercy,* engaging only in win-win relationships is the only path to success. *There is no victory if you win and I lose, or I win and you lose.* Tangible progress and happiness only exist when we share the bounty of our labor and prosperity.

"If you wish
mercy, show mercy
to the weak."

- Rumi

## *Mercy on the Enemy*

Wars, especially wars as destructive as World War II, are hardly the places for bold acts of compassion. Yet, one German soldier proved this idea to be wrong.

In 1943, German fighters had severely damaged the B-17 Flying Fortress (named Ye Olde Pub) under the control of Lieutenant Charlie Brown. The worst part was the damaged compass leading the plane to the enemy's territory.

Franz Stigler, the German pilot, was ordered to shoot down B-17 and destroy the enemy.

But as he got closer to the flying fortress, he saw that the plane was in a truly terrible state. He also saw how Brown was desperately trying to save himself from the dangerous situation that could end his life.

Franz Stigler could have destroyed Brown as he was ordered to, but instead, he decided to guide and escort the B-17 outside to a safe zone not occupied by the Germans. He even saluted Brown before heading back and telling everyone he had shot down the B-17 and the lieutenant he protected.

Almost 50 years later, Brown searched for his savior. When the two met again, they became friends and remained friends until Stigler passed away in March 2008, followed by Brown's death only a few months later.

Franz Stigler later said that he couldn't shoot Brown and his plane because they had flown beside each other for a long time, and Brown was desperate to return home. He saw the situation the same as shooting a man in a parachute.

Stigler's act of mercy was genuinely courageous. He could have easily destroyed the enemy and taken credit for it. Instead, he decided to protect a brave man who had fought his battle and now only wanted to return to a safe place.

He risked being found out and burdened with the blame of disobeying orders and saving someone considered the enemy. Instead, he decided to show mercy and prove that even the soldiers handling the most arduous tasks could have a big heart and show humanity.

https://mindsetopia.com/inspiring-stories-of-mercy/ by Saeed
Ahmadi

**Things to Ponder!**

"Mercy on the Enemy" serves as a reminder that life is complicated and certainly not black and white. *Merciful individuals possess robust moral values, integrity, empathy, and a sense of oneness with all.* They know of our shared need for love, fairness, compassion, and kindness. And that we live, flourish, and succeed as those around us do.

Am I comfortable giving and receiving mercy and compassion?

If "not," why not?

"*Those which disregard mercy, burn the bridge they will someday need to cross.*"

— HCJ

## *Sailing the Seas of Compassion*

Mercy Ships has been a ray of hope and rehabilitation for some of the most disadvantaged areas of the world ever since its modest beginnings in 1978.

This company stands out for its exact approach to delivering medical care—via hospital ships.

Mercy Ships has a fleet of state-of-the-art medical facility ships that are staffed by a dedicated group of volunteers that includes surgeons, nurses, doctors, and a variety of clinical specialties. These caring individuals, who come from all over the world, are motivated by the desire to significantly improve the lives of those without access to quality healthcare.

These floating hospitals travel to places with poor healthcare and deliver life-saving procedures, cutting-edge therapies, and healthcare instruction.

The organization's goal is to strengthen local healthcare systems, promote long-lasting change, and handle scientific situations.

Mercy Ships is renowned for its commitment to providing such services completely free of charge. It operates on the principle of compassion, holding that access to first-rate healthcare is a fundamental human right, regardless of one's socioeconomic status or location.

Mercy Ships has impacted many people's lives throughout the years by transforming testimonies of struggle and despair into tales of hope and healing. They have performed cleft lip and palate surgeries, treated crippling tumors, fixed crippling orthopedic disorders and many more procedures.

Patients who had previously faced unachievable suffering are brought closer to brighter, healthier futures with every surgery, treatment, and minute of care.

https://mindsetopia.com/inspiring-stories-of-mercy/ by Saeed Ahmadi

## Things to Ponder!

"Mercy Ships" modus operandi is an example of how sharing our time, talent, and treasure successfully impacts the lives of many.

*We do not thrive alone.* For most of us, the food we consume, the home we live in, the transportation we rely on, and the environment we are part of are by-products of previous investments made by others on our behalf.

275

The Essence of Winners – *Mercy* & Forgiveness

*Our duty and responsibility is simple: step up and pay it forward.*

How do I expand my mindset and learn to be my brother's keeper?

# Forgiveness

> *"Free at last, Free at last. Thank God almighty we are free at last."*
> - *Martin Luther King Jr.*

The word "*forgiveness*" and the act of forgiving is perhaps one of the most misunderstood actions we will encounter in our lives. Many go through an entire lifetime holding on to emotional hurt/s, grudge/s, or situation/s, which only serve to poison our being and rob us of our happiness.

To forgive is to pardon an offense or offender. To let go of resentment, anger, and revenge.[1]

The *funny* thing is that we do not have to live with the pain. We can realize that we are all a work in progress, making mistakes that can hurt us and others. And that the solution to conquering and absolving ourselves from our collective damaging acts is simply letting go and *forgiving* ourselves and others.

Now, many will say I can't do that. We would rather wallow in our misery, for it is the ignorance we ascribe to, instead of breaking free and understanding that *forgiveness is a personal act of emotional and intellectual freedom*. It does not mean excusing or forgetting the behavior but releasing the negative emotions tied to a person, event, or situation.

You need not be friends with those who hurt you. You hold yourself and others accountable for transgressions and consciously choose your happiness and well-being over debilitating burdens.

*"Forgiveness,*
*is the greatest gift*
*you can give yourself."*
*- Unknown*

## *Forgiveness of A Drunk Driver*

In February 2007, Chris Williams and his family got into a fatal accident. In that accident, Chris lost his 11-year-old son, his 9-year-old daughter, and his pregnant wife.

He witnessed his family leaving him one by one from this world. He was left with pain and grief.

Yet the thoughts Chris revealed of having in the moments of being in physical and spiritual pain, even before anyone could come to his rescue, were the thoughts that could easily shock so many people.

> *"Whoever has done this to us, I forgive them. I don't care what the circumstances were; I forgive them."*

The driver who caused the accident, a drunk 17-year-old teenager, was later found by the police. It is so easy not to drink while driving. To stop reckless behavior, we only should resist the urge.

So, it is safe to say that the drunk driver did not accidentally cause this tragic story but deliberately chose to risk his own and someone else's life. Even though Chris Williams kept his word, he forgave the driver and let go.

*What is worse than seeing your family's last breath with your own eyes?*

*What can be worse than watching your whole world crumble because someone was not smart enough not to drive with an unclear mind?*

Not many of us can handle this painful fate like Chris Williams. He showed a sense of mercy and *"forgiveness"* beyond comprehension.

*He could have ruined his life with anger and bitterness, but he decided to be a man beyond imagination.*

https://mindsetopia.com/inspiring-stories-of-mercy/ by Saeed Ahmadi

## Things to Ponder!

*"Forgiving"* can be very difficult, but it is life-changing. "Chris," the family man in the story, could have chosen to hold on to the hurt and pain caused by a reckless person who destroyed his family; instead, he gave us an inspiring story of mercy, forgiveness, and compassion.

The Essence of Winners – Mercy & *Forgiveness*

The desire to punish people who hurt one can be overwhelming and even sound pleasing. However, as previously mentioned, forgiveness does not mean that the offense or offender is ever forgotten or not held accountable.

Empowered individuals know the detrimental personal and collective harm of harboring ill feelings. *They say "no" to being filled with anger, hatred, and revenge, for in the end, nothing compensates for their loss or emptiness.* They actively choose not to allow the pain to foment and rob them of another second of life.

Am I a forgiving person? If not, why not?

# Duty, Freedom & Justice

> *"We never fail when we try to do our duty.*
> *We always fail when we neglect to do it."*
> - Robert Baden-Powell

*Duty*" is something one is expected to be a part of or accomplish by moral or lawful obligation. It is the responsibility or commitment to perform a particular task, action, or role. Duties can arise from societal expectations, ethical principles, legal requirements, or personal agreements. Within ethics, duty is often associated with moral obligations, suggesting that individuals have specific, universally binding duties, irrespective of personal desires or consequences.[1]

The aspects of duty we address here are accountability, respect, and reverence for self, family, friends, justice, and country. Over the last decades, too many in modern society have given up, discarded, or lost their sense of *duty*. It can be described as the erosion of a foundation. Without it, our collective lives, institutions, and country collapse like a deck of cards.

In many cases, it is not that people do not know right from wrong; it's that they are unwilling to put in the effort, stand up and assume responsibility, and honor others' rights or opinions. They would rather someone else do it.

It's a form of laziness leading to a lacking and unempowered life. We must again be taught or reminded at home, schools, and everywhere else that a successful, happy, and fulfilling quality of life is not without its cost. But that living a life shackled by mediocrity and discontent is a far heavier price to pay.

*Remember to always choose right over wrong and duty over laziness, and you will reap the fruits of your actions.*

"Duty, Honor, Country.
Those three hallowed words
reverently dictate what you
ought to be, what you can
be, what you will be."

- Douglas MacArthur

## *Great Duty*

Whenever a president travels, he is never alone. When the president is away from the White House, hundreds of personnel, including White House staff, Secret Service, and press reporters, are assigned to be on those flights and stay in hotels away from home and their families.

At Christmas, those requirements do not change. That is why President George W. Bush never traveled over Christmas during his eight years in office.

President Bush spent his Christmas holidays 60 miles from Washington D.C. at Camp David. Why? So his staff, the Secret Service, and the reporters assigned to him could wake up in their own beds on Christmas morning and be with their families.

In fact, President Clinton, the elder President Bush, and President Reagan all spent Christmas at Camp David or the White House for the exact same reason as George W. Bush. They felt it was their moral obligation to do that for those families.

Contrast that with recent history. For eight years of his presidency, President Obama spent Christmas in Hawaii. This past Christmas, President Trump spent

Christmas in Florida. As a result, hundreds of families were separated on Christmas morning. For the past 9 years, it has been the Duty of all those support personnel to spend their Christmas holidays away from their families. It's part of their assigned tasks. They really have no choice.

The president can make a choice, though. The president deserves a break at Christmas. The demands of being president are extraordinary. However, how much more astonishing is the great sense of duty of President George W. Bush and his predecessors?

https://www.andersonleadershipsolutions.com/short-story-great-duty-500-words/Apr.4, 2018

**Things to Ponder!**

We can all exercise our moral obligations. Putting the needs of others before our convenience, needs, or desires demonstrates a great sense of *"duty,"* respect, humility, and selflessness.

*The more faithful we are to our duties, the stronger our character and capacity to overcome, grow, and succeed.*

Do I live up to my duties and responsibilities?

If "Yes," how?

If "No," why not?

# Freedom

> *"This nation, under God, shall have a new birth of freedom — and that government of the people, by the people, for the people, shall not perish from the earth."*
> - Abraham Lincoln

In our country, "*freedom*" is enshrined in our constitution through amendments known as the "Bill of Rights." Specifically, Amendment I addresses freedom of religion, the right to assemble, and the right to speak.

It's a fundamental human right encompassing various aspects of life, including personal liberty, autonomy, and the capacity to make choices without undue influence or oppression. Freedom can manifest in many forms, such as freedom of speech, freedom of expression, freedom of thought, and the freedom to pursue one's aspirations and live according to one's values and beliefs.[1]

Take a deep breath; that is not free, nor is freedom. It has been paved by the sacrifice, injuries, and death of many of our predecessors.

Like it or not, it is our individual and collective responsibility to pay it forward to our future generations by investing in our people, science, technology, climate, and environment.

Ours is a finite planet with limited resources. Abuse or mishandle our freedom, and we as people, culture, country, and world are toast.

"For to be free is
not merely to cast off
one's chains, but to live
in a way that respects
and enhances the
freedom of others."
— Nelson Mandela

## *Finding the Meaning of Life*

Once upon a time, a man named Michael lived in an apartment in New York City. He was caught in a chaotic whirlwind of life. He was an average person, working nine to five to support his lifestyle.

He was struggling to find a meaning of liberty in his daily routine. *He was sad.* His life was like a monotonous cycle. He always wanted something more in his life. He wanted to become his own freedom fighter. One day, while browsing in a bookstore, Michael stumbled upon a self-help book.

The book's title was *"Actions do not cling to me because I am not attached to their results. Those who understand and practice this live in freedom."* He was intrigued by the title. He decided to read the book. He hoped to get enlightenment, the meaning of life.

Michael learned about the concept of *detachment* as he read the book. He found out about its impact on the interactionist perspective of a person. The author emphasized the importance of living in the *present moment.*

He found out about the outcome of our actions. It was a revelation to Michael. It was a key to breaking the chains of his existence. The book inspired Michael. He embarked on a journey to change his way of life.

He came to know that individual freedom was like a highway, and he should carefully drive his vehicle. He embraced the book's philosophy of how to live our lives fully. He was no longer like a mere spectator in his existence. He was now a protagonist in his life. *He understood that the absolute price of freedom was eternal vigilance.*

Michael started focusing on his work-life balance. He realized his job consumed his entire time. It was leaving little room for his fulfillment. With self-discipline, he carved out time for his hobbies.

He used it to revitalize his social life. Slow living became his mantra of living. He learned to savor each moment. He found joy in the little things which he used to ignore them.

His transformation was not limited there. Michael discovered the importance of self-care and nurturing his home life. He learned about believing in emancipation, which was the right of all sentient beings, and making his relationships strong. He cherished the love of his life. That fostered contentment inside him.

Michael found that his actions no longer clung to him as before. He continued to live his best life. He had let go of the need for validation. It urged him to be free from the suffering that attachment had brought into his life. *He realized that his results were not defining him and his character. It was the process — the journey — that mattered the most.*

Michael's *sad life* was now transformed into a life of purpose and *self-fulfillment.* Michael became an inspiration to others. Freedom was just another word for him. He radiated a positive energy that touched everyone. People admired his zest for life.

They were inspired by his ability to live in the present moment. Some people argued that freedom was never more than one generation, but they were not entirely authentic. His unwavering commitment to his happiness was his superpower.

Michael's tale spread far away, reaching every individual throughout the world. Like him, they wanted to be free from suffering.

It was the shackles that were holding them back from their fate. They embraced the concept of detachment. *They understood that the true meaning of life lies not in the destination but in the "journey" itself.*

Michael's anecdote became a lifeline for those people who were seeking change. They realized that they could rewrite the narrative of their life. The ripple effect of his transformation spread like wildfire. It ignited a movement of power among individuals.

*Michael understood that the meaning of life was not a fixed concept. Each person had to discover their liberation for themselves. It was found in detachment and embracing the present moment.*

He had found his own path of fulfillment. He found a way to be free from sin. He also gave courage to others, which helped them embark on their journeys *of "self-discovery and liberation."*

This circle of life actions no longer clung to Michael. He had indeed come to life. He reflected on his journey and *"realized that it was not about reaching a destination." It was about embracing the beauty of an unpredictable ride.* He prayed that all beings would be free from suffering.

The importance of *"freedom* was about living, *not just existing."* It was also about *"embracing the vast possibilities."* Michael had unlocked the true meaning of life. It was to create his inspirational short story about freedom in the great tapestry of existence.

https://medium.com/@subash761018/
5-freedom-story-in-english-finding-the-meaning-of-life-761ddd84f586

## Things to Ponder!

We are all searching to be free, liberated from our responsibilities and emotional and physical pain. We do not realize that what we need is *"freedom"* from attachments, which bind us to live an unhappy, restrictive, worrisome life.

What thoughts, obstacles, and concerns rob my happiness and constrict my freedom?
How can I change this?

# Justice

> *"Justice is the sum of all moral duty."*
> *- William Godwin*

For neons, people have construed their version of justice. Similar to "just-ice," which changes its form according to temperature from a solid to a liquid to vapor, justice can also differ on religious, social, and even lawful mandates depending on culture, government, or country.

*Justice* is a concept that encompasses fairness, equity, and moral rightness. It involves upholding rights and punishing wrongs according to the principles of law and morality. Justice seeks to ensure that individuals are treated fairly and their rights are respected within society.[1]

As previously alluded to, not all interpretations of moral or lawful conduct are agreed upon. Throughout our globe, different legal and ethical constraints or boundaries exist on how to dress or even what religion one practices, while in more liberal or open societies, nudity, same-sex unions, and diverse opinions are not only tolerated but encouraged.

At its core, though, regardless of where in the world we live or what parameters we are to adhere to, when we think or speak about justice, what we must want is a fair shot, an equal playing field, moral standards, laws, or rights, that we are all equally accountable to despite gender, race or personal affiliations.

Although, at times, failing to meet everyone's wishes, considerate and fair justice systems are the cornerstones of a *"prosperous"* people. Society adheres to and depends on their existence to progress and flourish, for they know that without, all that is left is anarchy.

"*Never*
*mistake law for justice.*
*Justice is an ideal, and*
*law is a tool.*"
- *L.E. Modesitt Jr.*

## *Justice, Love, and Mercy*

*Justice is not necessarily the law but the spirit of what is right and wrong,* but let justice roll down like waters and righteousness like an ever-flowing stream. (Amos 5:24) *Justice evolves and changes as it is applied with faith, values, and passion.* True justice is tempered with mercy and love.

Centuries ago, it was known far and wide that a certain leader was the greatest in all the tribes. When power was measured by proving superior physical strength, the most powerful tribe of all was the one that had the strongest leader who defined justice for the people.

But this tribal leader was also known for his wisdom. To help his people live safely and peacefully, he carefully put laws and a system of justice into place, guiding every aspect of tribal life. The leader enforced those laws strictly and had long ago acquired a reputation for uncompromising justice.

In spite of the laws, there were problems. One day, it came to the leader's attention that someone in the tribe was stealing. He called the people together.

*"You know that the laws are for your protection, to help you live safely and in peace,"* he reminded them, his eyes heavy with sadness because of his love for them. *"This stealing must stop. We all have what we need. The penalty has been increased from ten to twenty lashes from the whip for the person caught stealing."*

Then again, the thief continued to take things that didn't belong to him, so the leader called all the people together again.

*"Please hear me,"* he pled with them. *"This must stop. It hurts us all and makes us feel bad about each other. The penalty has been increased to thirty lashes."*

Still, the stealing continued. The leader gathered the people together once more.
*"Please, I'm begging you. For your sake, this has to stop. The pain it is causing among us is too great. The penalty has been increased to forty lashes from the whip."*

The people knew of their leader's great love for them, but only those closest to him saw the single tear make its way slowly down his face as he dismissed the gathering.

Finally, a man came to say the thief had been caught. The word had spread. Everyone had gathered to see who it was, and the thief was dragged through the crowd.

A single gasp raced through the crowd as the thief emerged between two guards. The tribal leader's face fell in shock and grief. The thief was his very own mother, old and frail.

What will he do? The people wondered aloud, a hushed murmur fanning out. Would he uphold the law, or would his love for his mother win over it? The people waited, murmuring, collectively holding their breath.

Finally, their leader spoke. *"My beloved people."* His voice broke. He continued in little more than a whisper, *"It is for our safety and our peace. There must be forty lashes; the pain this crime has caused is too great."*

With his nod, the guards led his mother forward. One gently removed her robe to expose a bony and crooked back. The appointed man stepped forward and began to unwind the whip.

At that exact moment, the leader stepped forward and removed his robe as well, exposing his broad shoulders, seasoned and solid. Tenderly, he wrapped his arms around his dear mother, shielding her with his own body.

He whispered gently against her cheek as his tears blended with hers. He nodded once more, and the whip came down again and again. *A single moment, yet in that moment, love and justice found an eternal harmony.*

https://projectshalom2.org/StoryTour/justice-love-and-mercy/ Posted 12/29/2020 by Rabbi

## Things to Ponder!

*"Justice"* is not an absolute system of laws and moral conceptions but the spirit of what is right and wrong. It changes and evolves depending on culture, faith, values, and beliefs. As the story on "Justice, Love, and Mercy" shares, true justice only exists when tempered with mercy and love.

*"When you love people, you hate the fact that they're being treated unjustly. Justice is not simply an abstract concept to regulate institutions, but also a fire in the bones to promote the well-being of all." -Cornell West.*

Have I ever been the victim of injustice? If "yes," how did I feel?

Have I participated in an unjust act? If "yes," how did I feel?

What is my definition of justice? Is it fair to all?

# Generosity, Abundance
# & Service

> *"We make a living by what we get.*
> *We make a life by what we give."*
> *- Winston Churchill*

*"Generosity, abundance, and service"* are about realizing that where we are in life is partly due to our efforts and, most notably, the endeavors, work, and achievements of others who paved our path.

We are the recipients of old and modern technology, infrastructure (roads, bridges, aqueducts, etc.), and educational and governmental systems that have facilitated, empowered, and fostered our lives. Consequently, it is our duty and responsibility to share our time, talent, and treasure as our ancestors did if we are to partake of further achievements and accomplishments.

We grow and prosper as the least of our brothers do, and amongst the most gratifying, fulfilling acts of generosity, abundance, and service for us is helping others prevail and thrive. Whether aware of it or not, our most empowering and noble role in life is to be our brethren's keepers.

Don't be scared and fall victim to the illusion, "What can I give? I barely have enough for myself" or "I am not Mother Theresa of Calcutta, India." Listening to your selfish, lacking-oriented ego is tantamount to disregarding our *abundant*, God-given nature.

Remember that our happiness, success, and fate are intertwined with everyone else's; we only triumph as they flourish and prosper. *Therefore, take ownership of your inherent nature, step up, and help someone in need! You will find it the most rewarding, joyous experience in life.*

As per the internet, _generosity_ is a quality characterized by a willingness to give or share, often without expecting anything in return. _Abundance_ refers to a plentiful quantity or supply, and _service_ is an act of helpful activity.

The *three* can be expressed through various forms of giving, such as *material gifts:* donating money, food, clothing, or other tangible items to those in need. *Volunteering your time* to help others through community service, mentoring, or simply being present for someone in need.

Giving *emotional support:* offering kindness, understanding, and encouragement to others, providing a listening ear or a shoulder to lean on. And Sharing *knowledge, skills, and* expertise to help others grow, learn, or achieve their goals.

Lastly, generosity, abundance, and acts of service are often driven by empathy, compassion, and a desire to improve the well-being of others. It strengthens communities, builds trust, empowers others, and creates a mutual support and cooperation culture.[1]

"Happiness doesn't result
from what we get, but
from what we give."

- Ben Carson

## *The Power of Giving*

About 26 years ago, Ilene Wright's Pastor was standing in line at a convenience store in New Orleans and noticed the family in front of him did not have enough money to pay for the few items they were buying. The pastor tapped the man on the shoulder and told him not to turn around but to please take the money he offered.

The man took the money and never turned around to look at the kind stranger helping them.

Nine years had passed since that incident in the convenience store, and the pastor was invited as a guest speaker in New Orleans. He spoke, and after the service, he stood by the door greeting people. After most of everyone had left, a gentleman walked up to him. He told the pastor an amazing story about how he had come to know the Lord.

Several years ago, he, his wife, and their child were destitute. They had lost everything, had no jobs, no money, and were living in their car. They were not Christians at the time and had decided to make a suicide pact, including the child.

They drove to a cliff and quietly discussed their fate. They decided that they should at least give their child some food before they killed themselves and left to buy him milk and food.

They were standing in line at the store and realized they did not have enough money to pay for the few little items they wanted to give their child for his last meal. Then, he said a man behind him spoke and asked him to please take the money from his hand and not look at him. The man also told him and his family that "Jesus loves you."

The man said they left the store, drove back to the cliff, and wept for 4 hours. They knew they could not follow their plan. The next Sunday, they drove by a church with a sign that said "Jesus loves you" and went in. The man and woman were both saved that day.

The man then told the Pastor that the minute he stood up in the pulpit and started speaking, he knew immediately that the Pastor was that kind stranger from 9 years ago. He said he would never forget that accent.

The Pastor is from South Africa and has a distinct accent. He continued telling the Pastor that because of his one random act, he saved three lives that day, and because he had told them that Jesus loves them, it had drawn them into a church where they accepted Christ!

https://www.city-data.com/forum/christianity/549297-very-touching-story-power-giving.html#ixzz25h0JvQk2

## Things to Ponder

Even though we seldom know the impact an act of kindness and *"generosity"* will have on someone in need, giving itself is rewarding and life-changing for the receiver and giver.

When we give without expecting anything in return, we affirm our infinite, empowering, and abundant oneness with all. Hence, inadvertently, we become the recipients of an understated, quiet, fulfilling happiness that is the reciprocal of giving.

The two-way street also reminds the receiver that they are not alone on their journey and that others care about their fate.

"When something is precious, instead of holding it tightly, we can open our hands and share it. We can share the wealth of this unfathomable human experience." - Pema Chodron.

Do I give?

If "yes," do I give anonymously, without expectation or attachment?

If I do not give, why not?

"Abundance is
about creating with your
thoughts and actions
a successful life."
- HCJ

# *Abundance Comes from Within*

Did you know that the greatest gift you can give yourself is the gift of abundance? Whatever it is you want—peace, joy, laughter, happiness, strength, a dream career, a better connection to Source, a deeper alignment with your higher self and life purpose—anything your heart desires can be attracted to your life with an abundant mindset and an open crown chakra. With this one shift, you can literally change everything!

## *The Source of Happiness*

You've probably noticed that there are people who seem to have it all: health, wealth, successful careers, marriages, partnerships, and most of all, they are honestly happy. *From the outside looking in, it may seem as though the material prosperity they've achieved created their happiness, but the truth is that it's usually the other way around.*

Internal perspective, clarity, and alignment with your soul purpose leads to external abundance. Abundance begins within you, with your thoughts and attitude, and with the proper mindset, there's no limit to what the universe can provide for you.

## *You Get What You Give*

The world is a closed circle; energy can't be created, only transformed, and every single thing on this planet is linked to every other thing through the unified field.

This means that you are connected to your neighbors and everyone else, to the physical earth, and to higher planes and Source, and what you do affects your personal energy as well as the energy around you.

You see this in little ways every day. Think about how easy it is to get sucked into someone else's bad mood when they're nearby—their energy can literally drag yours down.

But the reverse is true as well, and positive energy can also spread like energetic wildfire. In fact, that is what you are doing by studying energy healing and walking the path of light; you are helping to raise your own vibration, which raises the vibrations of those around you and, collectively, the universe at large.

This is no small thing—energy may be invisible, but it is more powerful than anything you can see with your eyes, and as it heals you, it heals the whole planet.

## *Ask, and You Shall Receive*

It is this same principle of interconnectedness that guides abundance. Your thoughts and emotions have their own energy, and what you think about and obsess about will eventually manifest. You give it weight by thinking and feeling about it so much. This has been proven in studies that show how effective prayer is.

Thought and emotion together push that energy out into the world where the desire can be formed and returned to you. Abundance is as simple as a consistent, meaningful request to the universe, accompanied by giving back what you hope to receive.

## *Shift Your Focus*

So, if you spend all your time thinking that you don't have enough money, the universe sees that as a request, and you will be provided with a continued absence of money. If you constantly lament the fact that you're not in a relationship, it will be hard to find one. If you are continually worried about getting sick, then the universe will provide you with an illness.

The universe will give you what you put your energy into, so if you want to manifest the good, you have to shift your focus and attitude.

If you want more money, start donating what you can spare. If you want more love, adopt a pet. Be of service without expectations. True abundance is an inner knowing that you are living the best version of yourself, so switch from focusing on the lack of what you want to focusing on bringing what you want into your life so you can be that best version.

Sometimes, I find students can't manifest their desires because they don't really believe they deserve them. If your thoughts contradict your emotions, the universe tends to hear your feelings. You may think you want more peace, but if you secretly feel you deserve to be punished for past mistakes, you will continue to be punished.

Energy healing techniques like meditation and journaling to release those negative emotions can help you adjust your thoughts toward the positive and allow you to attract the abundance you want and deserve.

## Open Your Crown Chakra

Another way to create internal abundance is to open your seventh chakra, which sits at the top of your head and is connected to thought, consciousness, information, and intelligence—all aspects of the process of knowing. When the seventh chakra is clear and balanced, divine energy can flow into it from the universal field, expanding your consciousness and providing you with a greater awareness of what you are truly meant to do. *With this knowledge, you then have the potential to manifest the life you want to have— the life you were born to live—and the abundance you seek.*

https://deborahking.com/abundance-comes-from-within/?v=7516fd43adaa

Deborah King

## Things to Ponder!

*"Abundance"* is a mindset that is promoted and sustained by our connection to a higher self. Still, for many of us, it seems that life's trials and tribulations contribute to forgetting that we partake of an infinite, bountiful source. But, as the story "Abundance Comes from Within" reminds us, living a life of abundance is readily available to us, with a slight change of our perception from lacking thoughts and attitudes to a generous disposition. It is not the amount we give that matters but the willingness to do it without judgment or expecting anything in return.

When was the last time I gave to or helped a stranger in need? How do I feel when I am generous with my time, talents, or treasure?

*"Unwise people think only of themselves, and the result is confusion and pain.*

*~~~*

*The wise know, the best they can do for themselves is to be there for others, and as a result they experience joy."*

*- Dalai Lama*

## *How to Be of Service*
### (And Why It Matters)

The best thing you can do for yourself and the planet is to be of service to others. You can practice every energy medicine technique in the book: journal your deepest feelings until your wrist hurts, meditate twice daily, pray, connect with Mother Nature, clear your chakras, release your limiting beliefs, etc., but if you aren't of service, you are not fully living in the light.

Being of service doesn't have to include the big gestures you might think about. You don't have to quit your job and give up your life to join volunteers in a far-off area to help disaster victims or donate your life savings to charity. You don't have to work at a food bank or with at-risk teens unless you want to.

Being of service is not only about what you do but also about how you do it. True service means doing what you are meant to do with compassion and love.

Understanding that service is both attitude and action helps you see that the opportunities for service are constant in everything you do. Let that car into the lane ahead of you, smile at the tired-looking bank or grocery store clerk, and offer to help someone with their hands full carry their drinks at Starbucks.

These gestures may seem small, but each one sends a ripple of love into the universe. And chances are, you will have uplifted the person you helped and possibly inspired them to also be of service, further stretching the reach of kindness and love. Enough ripples create a wave, and selfless service is the first step to spurring a wave of deep and boundless love to wash over the world.

# Here are a few additional tips for how to be of service:

### *Chop wood, carry water.*

This is the phrase I use in my energy healing courses and workshops to help teach my students that being of service means you have to do the work, get your hand dirty, so to speak.

Anything you do that gives of your time and energy to benefit someone else, as long as you do it with love and without expectation of reward, counts as being of service.

For you, this might mean planting trees in a neighborhood park, walking dogs, or playing violin on a busy street corner. Perhaps you're a birthday party clown, food server, or window washer. Service can be any deed or action that elevates others.

After all, that clown is making kids laugh. A restaurant server helps to feed customers. A street corner musician gives a little art to brighten the day of passersby. When you do your work from a place of light, that light radiates to everyone you interact with like a beacon of hope, compassion, and love.

### *Figure out how you would like to help.*

It's tough to act out of love if you're miserable, and serving others while resenting the work or the people will fill you with negativity rather than love, which doesn't help anyone. So, take the time to do some soul-searching and think about how you would like to serve others.

Try not to think about what your parents or partner think you should do. As much as possible, shut down any self-doubt that tells you you cannot do something and focus on getting in touch with your true feelings about what you want to do.

Journal about it, mull it over, ask your guides, and I bet you'll find that the way you want to serve takes advantage of your unique gifts. You were given your gifts for a reason, so use them! If you're great at organizing, wonderful with children, can paint portraits, or are a born counselor or energy healer, these talents are the way to serve authentically and without resentment or irritation. In this way, being of service can help awaken and strengthen your unique skills and help heal and uplift others.

I want to mention a rarely discussed truth about being of service: it's okay to enjoy it!

There seems to be the misconception that service must be somber and joyless, but who wants to be helped by someone who is all doom and gloom? Joy creates joy. If you are joyful in your service, everyone around you will also be buoyed by that happy energy.

## *Check your ego at the door.*

An expectation of reward is the greatest obstacle to true service. There are two types of giving: that which seeks recognition and that which serves in silence. If you are serving others so that you will be seen serving others, you are feeding your ego and not feeding the greater good. If you want to be known as a "good-doer" more than you want to do good, you are not truly being of service.

Even those in healing or helping professions, like doctors, therapists, or teachers, are only really being of service if they do those jobs in a compassionate, selfless manner.

A doctor who helps others solely to advance her personal power and greed is not embracing the attitude of love that genuine service requires.

Focusing on others without thinking of yourself is what makes service a spiritual practice; the process forces you to step outside your small, selfish, Earthly self and think of the greater interconnectedness of all life. As a spiritual teacher, this is an important lesson I teach. Since the universal field encompasses us all, what you send out into the universe comes back to you, so sending positivity to others also improves your life.

And, as a bonus, when you stop worrying about your own progress and success, that's when Spirit rewards you precisely that.

https://deborahking.com/how-to-be-of-service-and-why-it-matters/?v=7516fd43adaa Deborah King

**Things to Ponder**

Although seldom taught to us and sometimes forgotten, ours is a life made fulfilling, complete, and happy through *"service to others."* Our path to enlightenment, prosperity, and success is through lifting those in need.

As the story "How to Be of Service" mentions, being of service is our highest calling, *living in the light.*

It is an attitude, willingness, and desire to help others with our time, talent, and treasure.

The only thing required to be a person of service is *emotional health*. The ability to manage mental, relational, and purpose-relevant resources and to have agency over your emotions, brain, and life experiences.[3]

Am I of service to others? If "yes," how? If "not," why not? How can I grow in service to my loved ones, friends, community, or country?

[3] *Emotional health* includes *resilience*, which is being able to handle any emotion, both positive and negative. *Empathy means* connecting with people on a deeper level, forming meaningful relationships, having inner strength, having the courage to be real, vulnerable and showing the world who you are. *Self-awareness is* knowing that you can think for yourself, take responsibility, and intentionally decide what and how you want to do things; *contentment* is being happy with who and where you are in life.

# Wisdom

> *"Never mistake knowledge for wisdom.*
> *One helps you make a living; the other helps*
> *you make a life."*
> *- Sandra Carey*

Most of us recognize the virtue of *"wisdom"* yet wonder how those who exhibit it became so wise. Since birth, we go through life learning and acquiring knowledge. But as many know, when the rubber hits the road, many of our life-long instructions seem to fail us, sometimes during our most difficult times.

We ask ourselves why? The answer is that making decisions or choices without wisdom as the driving intuitive part of the equation will often lead us to failure.

*Wisdom* is a complex, multifaceted, lifelong process encompassing a deep understanding of life and the ability to make sound judgments and decisions. It goes beyond mere knowledge or intelligence and involves the application of experience, insight, and discernment to navigate situations and challenges effectively.[1]

## The Essence of Winners — *Wisdom*

*If we are to grow and succeed in our journey, it is imperative that we cultivate wisdom.* We do so by learning to be self-aware, humble, still, and quiet. Through observation, introspection, contemplation, and reflection. Only then can we genuinely differentiate between right or wrong, truthful or untruthful, the practical from the impractical, and respond with sound judgment and confidence.

Some will think this requires much effort, which they are unwilling to engage in. However, the ramifications of not doing so usually leave us living a more stressful, painful, and turbulent life. *Our choice forecasts our future.*

*"Knowledge speaks.*

*Wisdom Listens."*

*- Unknown*

# The Pencil

An old pencil maker took his newest pencil aside just before he packed him into a box. Imagining the little fellow as a person, he recalled a few things about the pencil.

*There are five things you need to know,* he said to his pencil, before I send you out into the world.

Remember these five things – never forget them – and you will become the best pencil you can be!

The first thing is to remember that you will be able to do many great things, but only if you put yourself in someone else's hands.

Occasionally, you will experience a painful sharpening, but remember that this will make you a better pencil.

Keep in mind that you will be able to correct any mistakes you might make along the way.

Fourth, the most important part of you is what's on the inside.

Finally, remember this, as well: upon every surface that you are used, you must leave your mark. No matter what else happens, you must continue to write.

The pencil listened to him and promised he would remember these five things so that he could live his life with heart and purpose. – Author Unknown

https://healthyspirituality.org/wisdom-stories/ By Jean Wise, 9/24/2019

## Things to Ponder!

As the story "The Pencil" shares, we must be willing to trust and work with others to better ourselves. Along the journey, we will encounter numerous problems, issues, afflictions, and pain. It's an integral part of human development and growth.

There will be mistakes, setbacks, and conflicts usually derived from our resistance or clinging to predetermine unfavorable, harmful, or pessimistic thoughts. We overcome most of these by understanding that inherent within most of our concerns and issues lies their solution. "The mind is like a parachute; it works best when open."

One must remember that our actual being is boundless and infinite and that we must give life our all.

Winners do not see insurmountable issues or problems. But opportunities for solutions to better their lives and the lives of others.

Lastly, *"wisdom"* is often as simple as discerning the essential, what matters from all else, and acting with conviction.

How can I grow and make wisdom the foundation for my actions?

*"Yesterday I was clever, so I wanted to change the world. Today I am wise, so I am changing myself."*

- Rumi

## *Precious Stone*

A wise woman traveling in the mountains found a precious stone in a stream. The next day, she met another traveler who was hungry, and the wise woman opened her bag to share her food. The hungry traveler saw the precious stone and asked the woman to give it to him.

She did so without hesitation. The traveler left, rejoicing in his good fortune. He knew the stone was worth enough to give him security for a lifetime. But a few days later, he came back to return the stone to the wise woman.

*"I've been thinking,"* he said, *"I know how valuable the stone is, but I give it back in the hope that you can give me something even more precious. Give me what you have within you that enabled you to give me something more precious. Give me what you have within you that enabled you to give me the stone."*
– Author Unknown

https://healthyspirituality.org/wisdom-stories/ By Jean Wise, 9/24/2019

**Things to Ponder!**

Life is not about never making mistakes but recognizing our errors, atoning, and moving forward. The more we do, the more we grow in wisdom, courage, and success.

How do I feel about my missteps?
Do I recognize my erred ways and correct them?
    If "no", why not?

# Life's Purpose

> "Life has been compared to a box of assorted chocolates; we never know what we are going to get."
>
> – Forest Gump

As Cherie Carter Scott points out in her book *"If Life is a Game, These are the Rules, for many, life is like a game in which we are never given instructions nor told the rules on how to play. We begin at "GO" and aimlessly make our way around the board, hoping we play it right. We do not know the objective of playing nor what it means to succeed."* There is little purpose but to survive and play another day.

This way of living serves only to leave us empty, disappointed, disenfranchised, unempowered, emotionally, physically, and spiritually ill. How can we change this?

*"Life's purpose"* often refers to the reason or meaning behind one's existence. It's the idea that individuals seek a deeper reason for their lives beyond mere existence. It surpasses thoughts and memories into concrete actions that fulfill personal goals, contribute to society, and lead to happiness.

The Essence of Winners – *Life's Purpose*

More often than not, *cultivating purpose within ourselves* is accomplished by awakening to the concept that change, turmoil, and hard times are lessons for us to learn from. And that within us lies the answer to our destiny.

As we explore, embrace, take ownership of, and learn from the lessons and teachings we are exposed to, we begin to understand that personally and collectively, intellectual, emotional, and spiritual growth and freedom are what life is all about. And that an accelerant to our development and well-being is empowering others along the way.

"The meaning of life is
to find your gift.
The purpose of life is to
give it away."

– Pablo Picasso

## *The Moonlit Prophecy*

The rain pounded against the ancient windows of the British Library as Professor Samuel Winslow meticulously examined an old manuscript.

His gray eyes flickered with a mix of excitement and apprehension. It was a stormy night, aptly reflecting the turmoil within his mind. The manuscript he held, rumored to be the lost Gospel of Judas, had the potential to change the course of history. It was said to contain not only a spiritual message but also a prophecy that could alter the future of mankind.

Samuel, a renowned biblical scholar, had dedicated his life to decoding ancient texts and uncovering their hidden truths. However, the task before him felt different, more significant. The words on the page seemed to beckon him, challenging him to uncover their secrets and embrace his destiny.

Driven by a sense of urgency, Samuel set off on a journey that would take him to the heart of Jerusalem, a city steeped in religious history and mysticism. Armed with his vast knowledge of the biblical texts, he explored the narrow streets and hidden corners, seeking clues that would unlock the mystery of the prophecy.

As he delved deeper into the labyrinthine streets, Samuel stumbled upon an ancient archaeological site. The site, known as the Temple Mount, had witnessed the rise and fall of empires throughout the ages. It was said to hold the key to unlocking the true meaning of the prophecy.

With each passing day, Samuel uncovered fragments of the prophecy scattered throughout the historical sites of Jerusalem. These fragments, intertwined with real events and places in history, painted a vivid picture of a future filled with uncertainty. The prophecy spoke of impending disasters and a world on the brink of destruction.

However, amidst the gloom and doom, a glimmer of hope emerged. The prophecy revealed that within the chaos lay the opportunity for individuals to forge their own destinies. It was a call to action, urging people to *"take ownership of their future"* despite the challenges that lay ahead.

Samuel's journey led him to a clandestine group known as the Guardians of Knowledge. This enigmatic organization comprised scholars, scientists, and philosophers united by their commitment to preserving ancient wisdom and guiding humanity toward a better future. The Guardians possessed a wealth of knowledge passed down through generations. They revealed that the prophecy had been hidden away to protect humanity from the immense power it held. But now, in the face of imminent danger, it was time for the prophecy to be unveiled and shared with the world.

United with the Guardians of Knowledge, Samuel embarked on a race against time to decipher the complete prophecy and share its spiritual message with the world. *As they pieced together the remaining fragments, Samuel realized that the true power of the prophecy lay not in predicting the future but in "empowering individuals to shape it."*

Realizing just how important this message was, Samuel unveiled the prophecy to the world. The message reverberated across nations, igniting a sense of purpose within individuals. People from all walks of life found the courage to overcome their fears, embrace their destiny, and work towards a brighter future.

The world stood at the edge of a profound transformation. The Moonlit Prophecy had served as a catalyst, inspiring humanity to take ownership of their future. As individuals embraced their destinies, hope spread like wildfire, sweeping away the darkness that had clouded their spirits. The lessons learned from the prophecy taught humanity that the path to a better future lay not in predictions but in *personal responsibility and collective action. The Moonlit Prophecy illuminated the power that resided within each individual to shape their own destiny.*

It taught them that *"no matter how daunting the challenges,"* they had the ability to overcome them and *"create a future filled with hope and purpose."*

In the aftermath of the prophecy's revelation, Samuel Winslow found himself at the center of a global movement. He became a beacon of inspiration, encouraging people to look within themselves and recognize their inherent potential. His journey had transformed him from a mere scholar into a catalyst for change.

The world began to witness a remarkable shift. Governments and organizations acknowledged the need to address pressing issues such as climate change, inequality, and social injustice. People from all walks of life actively engaged in initiatives that promoted sustainability, compassion, and the pursuit of knowledge.

The Guardians of Knowledge once shrouded in secrecy, emerged from the shadows and played a crucial role in guiding humanity towards a new era. They shared their wisdom and expertise, collaborating with governments, scientists, and spiritual leaders to create a harmonious balance between progress and preservation.

As the years passed, the impact of the Moonlit Prophecy continued to resonate. *The world experienced a renaissance of spirituality, where individuals sought meaning beyond material possessions.* People discovered solace in ancient philosophies, blending them with modern scientific advancements to forge a holistic understanding of the universe.

Samuel Winslow, now an elder statesman, dedicated his remaining years to education and mentorship.

He established academies and institutes, nurturing the minds of young scholars and encouraging them to embrace their passions, challenge the status quo, and contribute to the betterment of society.

The prophecy had proven that even in the face of dire predictions and uncertainty, humanity possessed the resilience to rise above adversity.

It had reminded them of their shared humanity and interconnectedness, fostering a sense of unity that transcended geographical and cultural boundaries.

And so, as the sun cast its golden rays upon the world, a new dawn emerged. The legacy of the Moonlit Prophecy lived on in the hearts and minds of individuals who chose to take ownership of their future.

They carried the spiritual message within them, a constant reminder of the power they held to shape their destiny and *"create a world filled with compassion, wisdom, and limitless possibilities."*

In the end, the Moonlit Prophecy was not just a story of mystery and intrigue but a tale of humankind's indomitable spirit. It whispered to those who listened, urging them to awaken their inner potential and choose their destiny. And in doing so, they discovered the true essence of their existence— "to *live a life of purpose*, courage, and profound significance."

https://spiritualgrowthevents.com/moonlit-prophecy-spiritual-story-about-destiny/

## Things to Ponder!

Who am I? What is my purpose in life? What does my future entail? These are questions many of us struggle to answer.

As per *"Life's Purpose"* and "The Moonlit Prophecy," we go a long way in answering these questions by taking "ownership" of our lives, that is, do our diligence and awaken to our boundless nature. Our destiny is not to be imposed by anyone else's agenda or wishes, but by the level of desire, motivation, and effort we put forth.

We empower our lives, reach our potential, and create for ourselves and others a life filled with hope, endless possibilities, and purpose as we seek to confront, learn from, and overcome our challenges, uncertainties, and hard times.

*A magnificent, abundant, fruitful life is up to us! That's the secret to success.* But then, somewhere within our subconsciousness, we have always known this to be. So there are no excuses. It's time to go to work, regain our power, and forge a grand life.

Knowing the secret to success, do I begin to claim my destiny? Or do I purposely let excuses, complacency, and laziness sabotage my future?

# Epilogue

As you have reached the end of my book, I hope you enjoyed it, found its content and message helpful, and share it with family, friends, and colleagues.

Remember, we are a work in progress, and applying as many of these shared principles into our lives will go a long way towards enjoying a fulfilled, happy, and prosperous journey.

Lastly, I will share with you that despite being wheelchair-bound for the entirety of my adult life, the result of a diving accident when I was nineteen, these far from complete tenets have been my guide to living an enriched, successful life, and one that is readily available to all who aspire to it.

Sincerely,
Herman Cajigas Jr.

# Contact Information

For additional information, pictures, videos, or special discounts on quantity purchases by corporations, educational institutions, associations, or groups, please use one of the following contact options below:

Herman Cajigas Jr.

## *The Essence of Winners*

### A Roadmap to Arriving!

P.O. Box 940551

Miami. FL 33194

Ph:   (305) 467-0485

Fax : (305) 220-2666

info@TheEssenceOfWinners.com

www.TheEssenceOfWinners.com

Other books by author

Triumphant Ride! By Permit Only – Autobiography
One Man's Successful Journey Despite
His Formidable Challenge
Triumphant Thoughts
Inspirational Thoughts and Reflections

# Contributing Sources

[1] Dictionary.com, ChatGPT